OXFORD IB DIPLOMA PROGRAMME

CW00542147

EXTENDED ESSAY

COURSE COMPANION

Kosta Lekanides

OXFORD
UNIVERSITY PRESS

OXFORD
UNIVERSITY PRESS

Great Clarendon Street, Oxford, OX2 6DP, United Kingdom

Oxford University Press is a department of the University of Oxford. It furthers the University's objective of excellence in research, scholarship, and education by publishing worldwide. Oxford is a registered trade mark of Oxford University Press in the UK and in certain other countries

British Library Cataloguing in Publication Data
Data available

978-0-19-837776-4

1 3 5 7 9 10 8 6 4 2

Paper used in the production of this book is a natural, recyclable product made from wood grown in sustainable forests. The manufacturing process conforms to the environmental regulations of the country of origin.

Printed in India

Acknowledgements

The publishers would like to thank the following for permissions to use their photographs:

Cover image: Alamy Stock Photo; p19: vkstudio/Alamy Stock Photo; p19: GL Archive/ Alamy Stock Photo; p41: John Greim/Getty images; p43: Hulton Archive/Getty images; p45: GL Archive / Alamy Stock Photo; p50: Xurxo Lobato/Getty images; p52: Alexei Zinin/ Shutterstock; p70: DEA / G. NIMATALLAH/Getty images; p73: World History Archive / Alamy Stock Photo; p96: The Print Collector/Print Collector/Getty Images; p97: M.Flynn / Alamy Stock Photo; p97: CM Dixon/Print Collector/Getty Images; p98: De Agostini / C. Sappa/ Getty images; p98: PRISMA ARCHIVO/Alamy Stock Photo; p99: Basphoto/Dreamstime.com/ licensed by OUP; p119: John Baran/Alamy Stock Photo; p121: Use of Microsoft Copyrighted Content ; p123: Permissions in progress; p121: Use of Microsoft Copyrighted Content ; p139: Sean Gallup/Staff/Getty images; Artwork by Thomson Digital and OUP.

Although we have made every effort to trace and contact all copyright holders before publication this has not been possible in all cases. If notified, the publisher will rectify any errors or omissions at the earliest opportunity.

Links to third party websites are provided by Oxford in good faith and for information only. Oxford disclaims any responsibility for the materials contained in any third party website referenced in this work.

Course Companion definition

The IB Diploma Programme Course Companions are resource materials designed to support students throughout their two-year Diploma Programme course of study in a particular subject. They will help students gain an understanding of what is expected from the study of an IB Diploma Programme subject while presenting content in a way that illustrates the purpose and aims of the IB. They reflect the philosophy and approach of the IB and encourage a deep understanding of each subject by making connections to wider issues and providing opportunities for critical thinking.

The books mirror the IB philosophy of viewing the curriculum in terms of a whole-course approach; the use of a wide range of resources, international mindedness, the IB learner profile and the IB Diploma Programme core requirements, theory of knowledge, the extended essay, and creativity, activity, service (CAS).

Each book can be used in conjunction with other materials and indeed, students of the IB are required and encouraged to draw conclusions from a variety of resources. Suggestions for additional and further reading are given in each book and suggestions for how to extend research are provided.

In addition, the Course Companions provide advice and guidance on the specific course assessment requirements and on academic honesty protocol. They are distinctive and authoritative without being prescriptive.

IB mission statement

The International Baccalaureate aims to develop inquiring, knowledgable and caring young people who help to create a better and more peaceful world through intercultural understanding and respect.

To this end the IB works with schools, governments and international organizations to develop challenging programmes of international education and rigorous assessment.

These programmes encourage students across the world to become active, compassionate, and lifelong learners who understand that other people, with their differences, can also be right.

The IB learner Profile

The aim of all IB programmes is to develop internationally minded people who, recognizing their common humanity and shared guardianship of the planet, help to create a better and more peaceful world. IB learners strive to be:

Inquirers They develop their natural curiosity. They acquire the skills necessary to conduct inquiry and research and show independence in learning. They actively enjoy learning and this love of learning will be sustained throughout their lives.

Knowledgable They explore concepts, ideas, and issues that have local and global significance. In so doing, they acquire in-depth knowledge and develop understanding across a broad and balanced range of disciplines.

Thinkers They exercise initiative in applying thinking skills critically and creatively to recognize and approach complex problems, and make reasoned, ethical decisions.

Communicators They understand and express ideas and information confidently and creatively in more than one language and in a variety of modes of communication. They work effectively and willingly in collaboration with others.

Principled They act with integrity and honesty, with a strong sense of fairness, justice, and respect for the dignity of the individual, groups, and communities. They take responsibility for their own actions and the consequences that accompany them.

Open-minded They understand and appreciate their own cultures and personal histories, and are open to the perspectives, values, and traditions of other individuals and communities. They are accustomed to seeking and evaluating a range of points of view, and are willing to grow from the experience.

Caring They show empathy, compassion, and respect towards the needs and feelings of others. They have a personal commitment to service, and act to make a positive difference to the lives of others and to the environment.

Risk-takers They approach unfamiliar situations and uncertainty with courage and forethought, and have the independence of spirit to explore new roles, ideas, and strategies. They are brave and articulate in defending their beliefs.

Balanced They understand the importance of intellectual, physical, and emotional balance to achieve personal well-being for themselves and others.

Reflective They give thoughtful consideration to their own learning and experience. They are able to assess and understand their strengths and limitations in order to support their learning and personal development.

A note on academic honesty

It is of vital importance to acknowledge and appropriately credit the owners of information when that information is used in your work. After all, owners of ideas (intellectual property) have property rights. To have an authentic piece of work, it must be based on your individual and original ideas with the work of others fully acknowledged. Therefore, all assignments, written or oral, completed for assessment must use your own language and expression. Where sources are used or referred to, whether in the form of direct quotation or paraphrase, such sources must be appropriately acknowledged.

How do I acknowledge the work of others?

The way that you acknowledge that you have used the ideas of other people is through the use of footnotes and bibliographies.

Footnotes (placed at the bottom of a page) or endnotes (placed at the end of a document) are to be provided when you quote or paraphrase from another document, or closely summarize the information provided in another document. You do not need to provide a footnote for information that is part of a 'body of knowledge'. That is, definitions do not need to be footnoted as they are part of the assumed knowledge.

Bibliographies should include a formal list of the resources that you used in your work. The listing should include all resources, including books, magazines, newspaper articles, Internet-based resources, CDs and works of art. 'Formal' means that you should use one of the several accepted forms of presentation. You must provide full information as to how a reader or viewer of your work can find the same information. A bibliography is compulsory in the extended essay.

What constitutes misconduct?

Misconduct is behaviour that results in, or may result in, you or any student gaining an unfair advantage in one or more assessment component. Misconduct includes plagiarism and collusion.

Plagiarism is defined as the representation of the ideas or work of another person as your own. The following are some of the ways to avoid plagiarism:

- Words and ideas of another person used to support one's arguments must be acknowledged.

- Passages that are quoted verbatim must be enclosed within quotation marks and acknowledged.

- CD-ROMs, email messages, web sites on the Internet, and any other electronic media must be treated in the same way as books and journals.

- The sources of all photographs, maps, illustrations, computer programs, data, graphs, audio-visual, and similar material must be acknowledged if they are not your own work.

- Works of art, whether music, film, dance, theatre arts, or visual arts, and where the creative use of a part of a work takes place, must be acknowledged.

Collusion is defined as supporting misconduct by another student. This includes:

- allowing your work to be copied or submitted for assessment by another student

- duplicating work for different assessment components and/or diploma requirements.

Other forms of misconduct include any action that gives you an unfair advantage or affects the results of another student. Examples include, taking unauthorized material into an examination room, misconduct during an examination, and falsifying a CAS record.

Contents

1: The basics

Extended Essay skills and attributes

An Extended Essay is intended to be an academic-style research paper on a topic of your choosing in one of the available IB subjects. As such, it is intended to adhere to certain formal guidelines which this Course Companion will support.

At its core, the Extended Essay is aim ed at cultivating or developing a range of skills and attributes, which can be mapped thus:

On top of these, one could argue that an Extended Essay compels students to act in an academically honest and ethical manner – both in terms of their approach to research and in the final production of the essay itself.

Extended Essay components

Extended Essay basic structure	
1. What does the Extended Essay comprise?	An academic piece of writing on a topic of your choosing.
	Bibliography of only the works cited in the essay itself using an acknowledged referencing style (for example, the American Psychological Association (APA) style or Modern Languages Association (MLA) style). For more see Chapter 7: Assessment on pages 115–31.
	Appendices (where applicable).
	Note: It is not mandatory for an examiner to read anything in an appendix; as such, this should only include information that acts as ancillary support to the essay (such as exemplar questionnaires) and should not include information that is integral to the flow or argument of the essay itself.
	Reflections on Planning and Progress Form (RPPF). For more see Chapter 7: Assessment on pages 133–8.

2. What should the maximum word count be?	The maximum word count is 4,000 (plus an additional 500 words for the Reflections on Planning and Progress Form that is submitted with the Extended Essay). **Note:** The essay should **not** be any longer than 4,000 words as any writing over this limit will not be read and thus could have a negative impact on all assessment criteria.
3. How many hours should be spent on it?	The IB recommends that you spend approximately 40 hours, spread out over the course of your IB studies.
4. On which subjects can the essay be written?	For a full list see pages 4–5.
5. What policies accompany it?	• Academic honesty • IB's ethical guidelines • Animal experimentation policy It is a mandatory requirement that all essays are academically honest (see Chapter 8 pages 139–43) and adhere to all ethical guidelines (see Chapter 2 pages 18–19) including those regarding animal experimentation policy as outlined by the IB.
6. How is it supervised?	The IB expects students to receive anything from three to five hours of in-school supervisory support towards the completion of their Extended Essay. A supervisor is expected to provide advice and support but not prescribe questions or edit any work produced. Your supervisor will also be expected to validate the authenticity of the work submitted by you to the IB by signing and dating the Reflections on Planning and Progress Form (RPPF). External supervision (that is, non-school-based) is possible under certain scenarios, although only an in-school supervisor can sign the forms. For more, see Chapter 6: Supervision on pages 78–100.
7. How is it submitted?	The Extended Essay will be digitally uploaded to the IB by the candidate or school. The IB Diploma Coordinator will help facilitate this upload. Extended Essays should be saved using any of the following file types: ✓ Microsoft Word file (DOC) ✓ Microsoft Word 2007/2010/2013 document (DOCX) ✓ Portable Document Format (PDF) ✓ Rich Text Format (RTF)
8. How is it assessed?	The Extended Essay is assessed in accordance with the following five criteria: • **A:** Focus and method (6 marks) • **B:** Knowledge and understanding (6 marks) • **C:** Critical thinking (12 marks) • **D:** Presentation (4 marks) • **E:** Engagement (6 marks) **Total Marks Awarded:** **34** For more on each criterion and how to best tackle them see Chapter 7: Assessment (pages 101–38)

9. How many IB points is it worth?	There are three points available for the combination of the Extended Essay and Theory of Knowledge. The additional points are allocated as follows:

TOK/EE	A	B	C	D	E
A	3	3	2	2	Failing Condition
B	3	2	2	1	Failing Condition
C	2	2	1	0	Failing Condition
D	2	1	0	0	Failing Condition
E	Failing Condition				

NOT TO BE INCLUDED:	✗ Candidate details, session number, school and supervisor's name and any identifying features on the title page. The digital upload will take care of the personal details.
	✗ Identifying marks (names, school names, candidate numbers and so forth) anywhere in the essay itself.
	✗ Audio-visual material (such as video recordings and sound clips), although images and screenshots are fine.

Extended Essay subject availability

All Extended Essays must be selected from the list of available IB subjects as seen in the table below. The list of available subjects is updated annually by the IB, so do check with your school's IB/EE Coordinator.

Tip

It is highly recommended that you write your Extended Essay in a subject that you are already studying as part of your IB Programme. This will ensure you:

- are able to employ the relevant methodologies associated with research in your chosen subject

- maintain an approach to research that adheres to the one outlined by the IB for that subject area

- have access to content that could support your investigation.

IB Subject Group	Subjects/Categories
Group 1: Studies in language and literature	All supported Language A subjects.
	Category 1: Studies of literary works (all works originally written in the target language of the Extended Essay).
	Category 2: Studies of literary works (at least one work written in the target language of the essay compared with works written in another language).
	Category 3: Studies in language (all works originally produced in the target language of the Essay).

Group 2: Language acquisition:	All supported Language B subjects.
	Classical Greek and Latin. **Category 1:** A specific analysis of the language (its use and structure), normally related to its cultural context or a specific text
	Category 2: (a) A socio-cultural analysis of the impact of a particular issue on the form or use of the language
	(b) An essay of a general cultural nature, based on specific cultural artifacts (see page 6 for more on artifacts).
	Category 3: An analysis of a literary type, based on a specific work(s) of literature exclusively written in the target language
Group 3: Individuals and societies:	Business management
	Economics
	Geography
	Global politics
	History
	Information technology in a global society
	Philosophy
	Psychology
	Social and cultural anthropology
	World religions
Group 4: Sciences	Biology
	Chemistry
	Computer science
	Design technology
	Physics
	Sports, exercise and health science
Group 5: Mathematics	Mathematics
Group 6: The arts	Dance
	Film
	Music
	Theatre
	Visual arts
Interdisciplinary subjects	Environmental systems and societies
	Literature and performance
	World Studies

Source: *Handbook of procedures for the Diploma Programme*, International Baccalaureate, 2016.

Artifacts in language B essays

When writing an essay on a Group 2 subject you have the option to write under the thematic heading of "Culture and society" (officially called "Category 2b"). Under this heading you can base your work on a "cultural artifact" – a term that often leads to confusion.

The following table provides a list of acceptable cultural artifacts:

Cultural artifacts	Not cultural artifacts
• Written documents	• Political events (elections, referendums)
• Newspapers	• Historical events
• Magazines	• Social movements (for example, riots)
• News headlines	• Social issues (unemployment, immigration, racism, school violence, the role of women in X country and so on)
• Articles	• Towns or regions ("travel guide" extended essays)
• Books (other than literary)	• (Minority) ethnic groups
• Cartoons	• Media trends
• Adverts	• Styles of music
• Leaflets, brochures or manifestos	• Sports
• Laws or policies	• Traditions
• Historical documents or records	• Institutions (such as school systems and political parties)
• Spoken documents	
• Screenplays	
• Radio or television programmes	
• Song lyrics	
• Interviews	
• Visual documents	
• Works of fine art	
• Architecture (buildings, monuments and so forth)	
• Films	
• Stamps	
• Cultural icons	
• Fashion items and accessories (as a manifestation of culture)	
• Food items, dishes (as a manifestation of culture)	
• Brands (as a manifestation of culture)	

Source: *IB Coordinator's Notes, IBO, September 2015.*

Extended Essay quiz

Divide into pairs and test your partner with the following quiz.

Questions
1. How many words can your Extended Essay be?
a. 5,000
b. 4,000
c. 3,000
d. no word limit
2. How many marks is it out of?
a. 30
b. 32
c. 34
d. 36
3. What is an RPPF?
a. A mandatory form that needs to be submitted to the IB with three reflections written by the student and signed by the supervisor
b. A mandatory form that includes the student's and supervisor's details along with the research question
c. A mandatory form that acts as the Extended Essay's cover page
d. An optional form that can be used to track a student's planning and progress at three key points decided upon by the supervisor and student
4. What is the correct approach to citations in an Extended Essay?
a. Cite all works read as background information and the actual ones used in the essay itself
b. Cite only the works used in the essay itself but not images or tables
c. Cite only the works used in the essay itself including images or tables
d. No need to cite any works as it's not a formal requirement
5. How many hours does the IB recommend that you spend on the Extended Essay as a whole?
a. No time limit set
b. 40
c. 24
d. 5
6. Which of the following statements is true with regards to the role of the supervisor?
a. They are not permitted to edit your work.
b. They are not permitted to set the research question for you to respond to.
c. They can offer you support in terms of planning your essay.
d. All of the above are true.

7. Which of the following can be considered a cultural artifact for Language B essays?

  a. a cartoon

  b. a newspaper

  c. an advert

  d. all of the above

8. Which three subjects are interdisciplinary in nature?

  a. Environmental systems and societies, Social and cultural anthropology, Global politics

  b. Environmental systems and societies, Literature and performance, Global politics

  c. Environmental systems and societies, Literature and performance, World studies

  d. Environmental systems and societies, Information technology in a global society, World studies

9. What is the key guideline to bear in mind with category 1 Language A essays?

  a. The texts analysed in the essay must have been originally written in the target language of the essay itself.

  b. The texts analysed in the essay must have been originally written in a different language to that of the essay itself.

  c. Avoid writing an Extended Essay on very common literary texts.

  d. There are no guidelines.

10. What should you not include in your final submission?

  a. Your name and school's name within the essay

  b. Audio-visual material (for example, a film clip)

  c. Your supervisor's name and school

  d. All of the above

11. Which criterion is/criteria are penalized if you exceed the word limit?

  a. Criteria A and B

  b. Criteria C and D

  c. Criterion D

  d. Potentially all of them

12. What are the five assessment criteria?

  a. Focus and method, knowledge and understanding, critical thinking, presentation, engagement

  b. Focus and method, knowledge and understanding, investigation, presentation, reflections

  c. Focus and method, knowledge and understanding, reasoned argument, presentation, engagement

  d. Focus and method, knowledge and understanding, analytical skills, language skills, reflections

Answers to the quiz can be found on page 144.

2: Getting started

All Extended Essays require you to formulate your own research question that will invite an investigation and can be meaningfully answered within the prescribed limit of 4,000 words.

Subject and topic

As a starting point **always** opt for topics that are of meaningful interest to you. Consider the following questions:

1. Which subjects have you really enjoyed?		
Subject A:	Subject B:	Subject C:
For example: English literature	History	Biology
2. Which *topic areas* or *themes* or *periods* have you been intrigued by within these subject areas?		
Topic(s), Theme(s) or Period(s)		
For example: • 19th-century novels	• Ancient Greece	• Micro-organisms
• Love	• Spartans	• Bacteria
• Relationships	• Greco-Persian wars	

Designing a research question

Once you've considered the above table you will have a starting point for the development of your research question.

For example, your first column may indicate that you are interested in writing an Extended Essay on the following:

> The theme of love and relationships in 19th-century novels

This, however, is quite a broad topic and so will need to be narrowed down in order to produce a **workable research question**.

A useful technique is to start applying "limiting factors" to the broad topic you've initially selected. Taking the example above, a limiting factor would emerge from asking, "Which novelist from the 19th century am I interested in?"

The answer to this will limit the scope of the investigation to a specific author(s) thus limiting the range from an initial and very broad topic (that is, 19th-century novels) to specific novelists from the 19th century.

The original title above could now be refined to this:

> The theme of love and relationships in the novels of Jane Austen

However, this is still too broad a basis for a research question as there are simply too many Austen novels to be able to successfully answer this

Terminology

Workable research question: A question with a clear focus that can be successfully answered within the given word limit.

within the word limit. Further questions would therefore need to be asked to help limit the scope of the investigation further.

As you will see in the table below, we can narrow down the scope of the investigation by taking each aspect of the question in turn and asking what the possible limiting factors could be (highlighted in yellow).

Terminology

Limiting factors: Relevant sub-areas for investigation that help limit the scope of one's research question.

Subject:	ENGLISH (Language A)
ORIGINAL TITLE:	
The theme of love and relationships in 19th-century novels	
Limiting factor:	19th-century novels
Question:	Which novels or novelists from the 19th century am I interested in?
Answer:	Jane Austen

REFINED TITLE:	
The theme of love and relationships in the novels of Jane Austen	
Limiting factor:	Jane Austen
Question:	Which specific work(s) by Austen?
Answer:	*Pride and Prejudice*

REFINED TITLE:	
The theme of love and relationships in *Pride and Prejudice*	
Limiting factor:	Relationships
Question:	What type of relationships?
Answer:	Married/Unmarried

REFINED TITLE:
Austen's attitudes to love and marriage in *Pride and Prejudice*

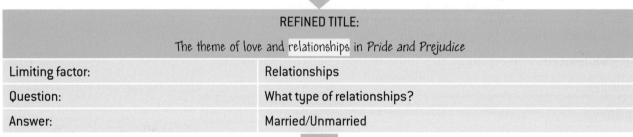

FINAL QUESTION
In what ways does Jane Austen express her attitudes to the themes of love and marriage inherent in her work *Pride and Prejudice*?

The above refined title is a very good starting point to begin your Extended Essay research as it has a clear focus and is narrow enough to be covered within the word limit.

Below are further examples of how one can apply limiting factors to a variety of subject-specific titles:

Subject:	History
ORIGINAL TITLE:	
Authoritarian states of the 20th century	
Limiting factor:	Authoritarian states
Question:	Which authoritarian states am I interested in?
Answer:	Communism under Stalin, Fascism under Mussolini

REFINED TITLE:	
A comparison of the communist state in Russia under Stalin with the fascist state of Italy under Benito Mussolini.	
Limiting Factor:	Comparison, communist state, fascist state
Question:	Which specific area of these two states am I interested in comparing?
Answer:	Who was more effective in controlling their citizens

REFINED TITLE:
To what extent was Stalin's communist state more effective than Mussolini's fascist state in controlling its citizens?

Subject:	Visual arts
ORIGINAL TITLE:	
The architecture of Le Corbusier	
Limiting factor:	Architecture
Question:	What specific architecture from Le Corbusier's work am I interested in?
Answer:	Villa Stein (Garches, France), Unité d'Habitation (Marseilles, France)

REFINED TITLE:	
An exploration into the works Villa Stein and Unité d'Habitation by architect Le Corbusier.	
Limiting Factor:	Villa Stein (Garches, France), Unité d'Habitation (Marseilles, France)
Question:	Which specific aspect of these buildings do I want to explore?
Answer:	The use of proportional systems such as Le Corbusier's "Modulor"

REFINED TITLE:
In what ways does Le Corbusier utilize the Modulor proportional system in the works Villa Stein and Unité d'Habitation?

Subject:	Psychology
ORIGINAL TITLE:	
The usefulness of music therapy	
Limiting factor:	Usefulness
Question:	Useful in what manner or in what field?
Answer:	As a palliative for dementia sufferers

REFINED TITLE:	
An evaluation of the success of music therapy as a palliative for sufferers of dementia.	
Limiting factor:	Dementia
Question:	Which specific type of dementia do you wish to explore?
Answer:	Dementia of the Alzheimer's Type (DAT)

REFINED TITLE:
To what extent can music therapy be deemed a successful palliative for the symptoms of Dementia of the Alzheimer's Type (DAT)?

Limiting factors

Below is a list of general terms that allow for the narrowing down (or "limiting") of potential research questions. They are all accompanied by examples showing how a question can be more sharply focused when the general terms (in red) are narrowed down by asking "limiting" questions (highlighted in green).

Accuracy

Accurate in determining what exactly?	
Original question	How accurate are baseline tests such as Advanced Level Information System (Alis) or Middle Years Information System (MidYIS) in education?
Revised question	To what extent can baseline tests such as Alis be seen as an accurate means of determining student performance at IB?

Aspect

Is there a specific aspect that could be investigated (for example, a particular military confrontation, a specific programme, a type of therapy or a specific law)?	
Original question	How effective was Nazi propaganda in controlling its people?
Revised question	How effective was Nazi Youth propaganda in terms of indoctrinating German citizens aged 14–18?

Author

Which specific author/artist/scientist did you have in mind?	
Original question	How influential was religious iconography in the development of abstract art?
Revised question	To what extent does the religious iconography of the Orthodox Church shape the Composition series by Wassily Kandinsky?

Case study

Which case study did you wish to explore?	
Original question	Can studies on language conclusively show the impact of language on memory recall?
Revised question	How conclusive is the Loftus and Palmer study when it comes to determining the effect of language on memory recall?

Cause

Is there a specific cause of what you are trying to ascertain or measure (for example, an event, a person or group, or a chemical)?	
Original question	The re-election of Margaret Thatcher and her Conservative Party in 1983
Revised question	To what extent did the Falklands War help Margaret Thatcher secure the 1983 elections for the Conservative Party?

Effect

Is there a specific effect you are trying to ascertain or measure (for example, on behaviour or in terms of migration patterns or development of laws)?	
Original question	What accounts for decreased levels of intelligence among the young?
Revised question	To what extent can high levels of fluoride be seen as a major cause of decreased intelligence levels among children aged 5–10?

Effectiveness

What exactly are you referring to by "effective"? Effective in what way?	
Original question	The effectiveness of mental toughness among American Football players
Revised question	To what extent can mental toughness improve the athletic performance of American Football players?

Experiment

Which experiment do you wish to explore or question the validity of?	
Original question	Can an experiment in psychology ever be objective?
Revised question	To what extent can Benjamin Libet's experiments on free will be deemed objective?

Factors

Which specific factor do you want to focus on (for example, military, economic, social, cultural, religious, upbringing or nurturing)?	
Original question	The Greek victory over the Persians from 480 to 479 BC
Revised question	To what extent was the Battle of Thermopylae the most significant factor in the Greek victory over the Persians?

Features

Which specific feature do you wish to explore in your essay (for example, compositional, database or connectivity)?	
Original question	In-flight services provided by a major airline
Revised question	To what extent does the introduction of the Tempus system on X airline improve in-flight health care?

Location

Which country, city or location do you want to investigate?	
Original question	Implementation of Ravenstein's migration laws
Revised question	To what extent can Ravenstein's migration laws be applied to Dubai in the United Arab Emirates?

Material

Is there a specific material that lends itself well to your investigation (for example, a specific chemical, a metallic substance or a piece of technology)?	
Original question	The rate of enamel decay as a result of drinking orange juice as compared to whitening toothpastes
Revised question	The concentration of citric acid found in orange juice is more effective at stripping tooth enamel than the peroxide found in whitening toothpaste?

Methodology

Is there a specific method you want to investigate in terms of your approach?	
Original question	Which method works best for determining cash-flow optimization in the banking sector?
Revised question	How effective is the Taguchi method in determining optimal cash-flow levels in the banking sector?

Process

Is there a specific process or model that you could refer to? (for example, a specific model, research model or interpretation model)	
Original question	Company X's business model in improving sales between 2000 and 2005.
Revised question	To what extent did the change from a business-to-business model to a business-to-consumer model help improve sales for company X from 2000 to 2005?

Reliability

Reliable in determining what or when compared to what exactly?	
Original question	The reliability of meteorological (weather) forecast models
Revised question	To what extent can the use of Model Output Statistics produce reliable results when it comes to making hurricane predictions?

School

Is there a specific school of thought or movement you had in mind on which to base your interpretation or reading?	
Original question	A closer reading of William Faulkner's As I Lay Dying.
Revised question	In what ways can William Faulkner's novel As I Lay Dying be seen as representative of the Cubist Movement?

Skills

Which specific skill(s) did you wish to explore? (for example, numeracy, literacy or computational)	
Original question	Use of interactive software in classroom learning
Revised question	In what ways does the use of e-learning platforms such as X improve the literacy skills of students aged 5-10?

Society

Is there a specific type of social structure you'd like to explore? (such as patriarchal, matriarchal or industrial)	
Original question	Conflict between traditional and contemporary wedding practices in India
Revised question	To what extent can contemporary wedding practices in India be deemed a break from the patriarchal principles enshrined in the Manuvad system?

Technique

Is there a specific technique you want to investigate in terms of your approach?	
Original question	The theme of sexuality as seen in Syd Brak's "Kiss" series of work?
Revised question	To what extent does the use of airbrush techniques enhance the theme of sexuality in Syd Brak's "Kiss" n series?

Texts

Which specific text did you have in mind to focus your investigation on?	
Original question	Representations of autism in contemporary literature
Revised question	In what ways does Mark Haddon use the first-person perspective to represent autism in his novel The Curious Incident of the Dog in the Night-Time?

Time period

Which specific period in time did you want to investigate (for example, early years, defined period such as a decade or a specific event in time)?	
Original question	Impact of the White Australia Policy on Australia's economy
Revised question	To what extent was the implementation of the White Australia Policy in 1901 detrimental to Federated Australia's economical development from 1901 to 1920?

Type

Is there a specific product, version or design you have in mind?	
Original question	The ergonomic design of modern-day console controllers
Revised question	How have ergonomic factors been considered in the design of the PlayStation 4 controller to maximize first-person shooter (FPS) gameplay efficiency?

Comparisons

Occasionally, in the process of researching and reading for your selected title, you may discover that it easily accommodates a comparative that will lend the essay a more robust investigative focus. There is absolutely nothing wrong with expanding the reach of your essay to include a comparison, provided that a meaningful comparison can be made within the word limit.

> **Tip**
>
> If your essay's original research question is proving to be too narrow, consider adding a comparative element.

For example, in the English (Language A) question used above, the comparative element could alter the title to the following:

> How do Jane Austen and Helen Fielding express differing attitudes towards the themes of love and marriage inherent in their respective works *Pride and Prejudice* and *Bridget Jones's Diary?*

Another option would have been to compare two novels by Austen, provided they showed some difference in terms of how she approached the theme of love and marriage (for example, a work from her earlier years compared to one written much later in her life, when her attitudes may have changed with time).

Below are examples of the comparative element added to a research question in biology and history:

Biology – Non-comparative	To what extent do natural products reduce the growth of normal microflora (*Candida albicans* and *Streptococcus mutans*) in the oral cavity?
Biology – Comparative	To what extent do natural products reduce the growth of normal microflora (*Candida albicans* and *Streptococcus mutans*) in the oral cavity and differ in effect to commercial mouthwashes?
History – Non-comparative	To what extent could Anna Komnene's account of the First Crusade in her history the *Alexiad* be considered reliable?
History – Comparative	To what extent could Anna Komnene's the *Alexiad* and William of Tyre's *Historia* be considered reliable accounts of the First Crusade?

Question vs. title

Prior to the introduction of the new Extended Essay criteria in 2016, it was possible to state your research question in the form of a proposition, hypothesis or statement that invites an exploration. This would mean that your research question would be written up as a **title**.

This is **no longer** the case when it comes to Extended Essays. The new rules are quite clear on this matter and as such **all** Extended Essays must contain a research question written up as a question as opposed to a title.

However, this does not mean that when it comes to designing your research question you cannot begin with a title or hypothesis, provided that the finished version is in the form of a question.

Below is an example of how a working title in an English (Language A) Extended Essay could be converted into a question:

Title format:	The subversion of the archetypal depictions and classifications of the "hero" in George RR Martin's novel *A Game of Thrones*.
Question format:	How does George RR Martin subvert the archetypal depictions and classifications of the "hero" in his novel *A Game of Thrones*?

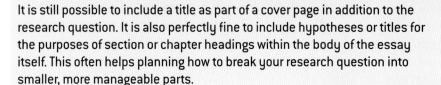

Special note

It is still possible to include a title as part of a cover page in addition to the research question. It is also perfectly fine to include hypotheses or titles for the purposes of section or chapter headings within the body of the essay itself. This often helps planning how to break your research question into smaller, more manageable parts.

Question starters

Below is a list of common question starters that may help you design your own research question or convert a working title into a question format.

Question starter	Description
To what extent ...	Allows for an evaluation of the degree (extent) to which something is true or a contributing factor. To effectively answer this type of question, the main body of the essay should include considerations of other influencing factors. For example, a question relating to the extent to which the Spanish Constitution of 1931 caused the civil war of 1936 could potentially examine the role played by the military, external nations and other factors in order to more fully answer "the extent" aspect of the question.
Assess the role of ...	Allows for an analysis of a specific factor or the contribution of something/someone.
How accurate/reliable ...	Allows for an exploration relating to accuracy or usefulness.
How far could one argue ...	Allows for the analysis to focus on the accuracy/truthfulness of a specific argument or line of enquiry.
How successful ...	Allows for an evaluation of the success of an approach, method, policy, style and so on an associated area (for example, success of a political policy on economic development of X region).
How crucial/significant ...	Allows for an analysis of the significance of one or more factors on other associated areas.
Which factors played ...	Allows for an investigation around key factors.
Has the introduction (or cancellation) of ... resulted in ...	Allows for a cause/effect-style investigation.
Does [X] process/approach provide ...	Allows for a focused investigation on the result of a specific method followed or technique used.
What is the contribution/influence of ...	Allows for a focused investigation on the impact (positive or negative) of a certain individual, group, material or concept on a broader area (for example, on a specific society).
What evidence is there to support ...	Allows for an investigation into the nature of evidence and the extent to which it can support a thesis or approach.
What is the impact of ...	A straightforward causal investigation.
Is it possible to determine ...	An investigation into hypothetical frameworks based on existing and available evidence.
Under what circumstances may ...	Allows an investigation into the conditions required before X is deemed possible (for example, for a business to expand).
Is there a correlation between ...	Allows for an investigation into the relationship between two or more factors.

Feasibility

Having a good research question is very important; however, equally as important is ensuring that this question is feasible. In order to evaluate the feasibility of a question it should meet a series of requirements including materials, equipment access and ethical guidelines, all of which will be outlined below. The key concern here is that the best questions do not always make the best Extended Essays if they cannot be researched effectively.

Remember

The best questions do not always make the best Extended Essays if they cannot be researched effectively.

Locating sources

Once you have arrived at a workable research question (or title) the next step is to see if you can **find and access** enough source material to begin your research investigation proper. This often takes the form of locating either primary or secondary sources (or a combination of both, in some instances) which will form the initial, core body of your work. This material will be the base of your analysis while simultaneously acting as an indication of whether such an investigation is feasible in the first place.

As a rule of thumb it is useful to identify at least **5–10 sources** that relate to your research question (or title) in order to ensure that the question is feasible. This is not a hard-and-fast rule, but it is useful in a number of ways:

- proving to yourself (and your potential supervisor) the feasibility of your question

- providing a starting basis for your investigation

- situating your work in a wider body of research.

Having said this, not every Extended Essay subject requires the use of primary or secondary sources. Refer to Chapter 3 for more support with locating suitable source material for an Extended Essay, along with a list of subjects and the degree to which each requires either primary or secondary (or both) source material.

Tip

Try to locate at least 5–10 sources relating to your research question to prove its feasibility.

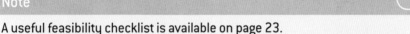

Note

A useful feasibility checklist is available on page 23.

Ethical guidelines for Extended Essays research and fieldwork

- Extended Essay students must exercise the greatest sensitivity to local and international cultures.

- Any research/fieldwork that creates anxiety, stress, pain or discomfort for participants is not permitted.

- Any research/fieldwork that involves unjustified deception, involuntary participation or invasion of privacy, including inappropriate use of information technology (IT), email and the internet, is prohibited.

- All participants in research activities must be informed before commencing the research that they have the right to withdraw at any time. Pressure must not be placed on any individual participant to continue with the investigation beyond this point.

- Each participant must be informed of the aims and objectives of the research and in addition be shown the results of the research.

- Informed consent should be obtained from the people who are the subject of the fieldwork. Research involving children needs the written consent of parent(s) or guardian(s). Students must ensure that parents are fully informed about the implications for children who take part in such research. Where research is conducted with children in a school, the written consent of the teachers concerned must also be obtained.

- Extended Essay students must avoid conducting research with any adult who is not in a fit state of mind and cannot respond freely and independently.

- If any participant shows stress and/or pain at any stage of the research, the research must finish immediately, and the participant must be allowed to withdraw.

- Participants must be debriefed and given the right to withdraw their own personal data and responses. Anonymity for each participant must be guaranteed.
- All data collected must be kept in a confidential and responsible manner and not divulged to any other person.
- Research that is conducted online, using IT methods, is subject to the same guidelines. Any data collected online must be deleted once the research has been completed. Such data must not be used for any purpose other than the conduct of the research.

– IB Ethical Guidelines, International Baccalaureate Organization, 2011

Disproving a research question

Many students often worry that their questions must be framed in a manner that can be positively proven, that is to say, the key thesis contained in their question must be correct.

For example, if I want to write a History Extended Essay on the American War of Independence, I may opt for a question such as:

> To what extent was George Washington's leadership a key factor in the American victory during the American War of Independence (1775–83)?

Even though there were certainly other factors, the conclusion to this question will more or less agree with the main thesis contained within it (that is, that Washington was indeed a key factor behind the American victory). Naturally, there is nothing wrong with a question like this, but you should not be afraid to explore alternative theses that your essay could disprove.

For example, taking the same historical episode, an alternate question could be:

> To what extent was the French and Spanish entry into the American War of Independence from 1778 to 1779 the key factor behind the final American victory in 1783?

Here we are presented with an apparent negative in that the French and Spanish contributions were not the key factors per se and thus we may reject using such a question because our conclusion will end up disproving the question's key thesis.

However, there is nothing wrong with doing exactly that in your Extended Essay as it shows the hallmarks of good research. If you pursued an essay such as this, you could mention the Franco-Spanish contributions followed by all the other factors that played a part in the American victory (for example, Washington's leadership, the geography, British mistakes, economic factors and military manoeuvres) before concluding that the War of Independence was won due to a variety of factors. In your conclusion you can assess the degree to which the Franco-Spanish contributions could be deemed "key" when compared against the other factors raised in the body of your essay. Provided this evaluation was present, this type of question opens up many opportunities for focused analysis and reasoned assessment.

Remember that one of the central pillars of the IB's Extended Essay is for students to wrestle with all the associated aspects of independent research and this often entails proposing theses that end up being disproven. Academic circles often seek to disprove, as well as prove, hypothesis in order to push knowledge a little further on. The key is to provide proof either affirming or disproving your thesis and not to worry if you end up disagreeing with your question's main thesis.

Changing your research question

1. **Change of subject and topic:** You may find yourself changing your research question quite a bit as your interests shift or as you encounter obstacles—usually in the shape of a lack of resources. As a result, you may find yourself wishing to change topics and/or subjects completely. This is perfectly normal state of affairs, however, **you should set yourself a cut-off point** after which no more changes are permissible. This will ensure that the work needed to be done for the Extended Essay can be completed without it affecting other assessments that will inevitably be due as part of the IB programme you are studying.

Tip

It is recommended that you avoid changing your subject and topic after the first six months of your first year of IB studies as you will find yourself well behind in terms of preparation.

Each school will inevitably have different logistical considerations to wrestle with (such as supervisor availability and assessment calendars) so cut-off points may already be set by the school. It is always important to stick with these as your school has its own process through which it engages the Extended Essay. The general consensus is that if a student does not have a fixed research question within the first six months of their IB studies, then this will add significant pressure on them to complete the Extended Essay once you factor in all their other Diploma or Course obligations. This does not mean, however, that tweaking and adjustments to a question are not possible throughout the process of writing your Extended Essay (more on this below).

2. **Adjustments to the research question:** It is quite common, and even advisable, to constantly re-evaluate your research question in light of the reading and research you conduct on your topic. The reading and research phase will inevitably open up new pathways that you may not have considered previously, or it may shed new light on a different approach that can be followed.

The key thing to remember is that your research question should:

a. reflect what your essay actually is about

b. be the question your conclusion responds to.

Essays often lose marks because the question on the cover is not exactly what the student has ended up writing about in the body of the essay or, most commonly, what the student has responded to in their conclusion. The best way to avoid this mismatch from occurring is to adjust your

Top tip

Adding a note in your Researcher's Reflection Space and then again reflecting on this change in your RPPF is also highly recommended as it will demonstrate the perfectly natural process of refining and re-evaluating that occurs with all research-oriented investigations.

research question to match what you **actually** wrote about in the end. Re-read you essay and if you feel the analysis has shifted to a different focus (however slight) then go back and reverse engineer your research question to match it.

Case study

John's initial research question was:

Which factor best explains Pharaoh Hatshepsut's rise to power in 1478 BC?

However, as he began researching and reading on the female Pharaoh he discovered that there was a lot more to be said for her consolidation of power as opposed to her rise to power.

The question was thus adapted midway through his research to read:

Which factor best explains Pharaoh Hatshepsut's consolidation of power from 1478 to 1458 BC?

Once the essay was near completion, John noted that his essay leaned heavily on Hatshepsut's use of religious and diplomatic propaganda to gain control over Egypt and that this was in fact the underlying thread throughout the essay. The question was thus adapted again to read:

To what extent can Hatshepsut's use of religious and diplomatic propaganda be considered the key factor behind her consolidation of power from 1478 to 1458 BC?

The key here is that the reading, research and eventual writing of the essay shaped the final research question so that the entire process was organic in nature, changing and adapting to suit where the work John did was taking him.

Worksheet: Design your own research question

A. General areas of interest

1. Which subjects have you really enjoyed?		
Subject A:	Subject B:	Subject C:

2. Which *topic areas* or *themes* or *periods* have you been intrigued by within these subject areas?		
Topic(s), Theme(s) or Period(s)	Topic(s), Theme(s) or Period(s)	Topic(s), Theme(s) or Period(s)

B. Applying limiting factors

Use the tables below as needed to refine your original titles into a workable research question. Refer to pages 10–12 for examples as to how this can be done. Please note that you must end up with a question and not a title as per the new IB rules governing the Extended Essay (2016 onwards).

Subject:	
Original question/title	
Limiting factor: Highlight or list the terms that can be limited.	
Refined question/title	
Limiting factor: Highlight or list the terms that can be limited.	
Refined question/title	
Limiting factor: Highlight or list the terms that can be limited.	
Refined question:	

C. Feasibility check

Does your research question pass the following feasibility checks?

Feasibility check	Tick
1. Are there sufficient primary sources available (if appropriate)?	
2. Are there sufficient secondary sources available (if appropriate)?	
3. Can you access the sources in your location?	
4. Do you have all the materials necessary to carry out your investigation at hand (for example, chemicals)?	
5. Do you have all the equipment necessary to carry out your investigation at hand (for example, lab or computer equipment)?	
6. Can you access the materials and equipment in your location (that is, have you gained necessary permissions)?	
7. Can you begin your research immediately (for example, you do not need to defer your research until the summer when you will visit X or Y place)?	
8. Your research question (or title) can be assessed against the Extended Essay criteria? See Chapter 7: Assessment for more on pages 101–38.	
9. The chosen research methods or concepts underpinning your research question are relevant and appropriate to the subject?	
10. Does your research meet all of the IB's ethical guidelines on research and fieldwork? (See pages 18–19 for the list of guidelines.)	

3: Locating, organizing and evaluating

Following on from the chapter on defining a research question, this section is designed to help students and supervisors locate, organize and evaluate the myriad of research that will be an integral part of the Extended Essay process.

The four-step process is outlined in the diagram below:

Step 1: Defining a research question

Step 2: Locating relevant sources to support research into the chosen topic

Step 3: Organizing the information into workable formats

Step 4: Evaluating in the light of such criteria as reliability, limitations and issues raised

Each part of the process will be covered separately in the pages to follow.

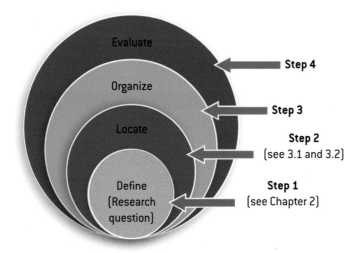

Primary and secondary sources

After designing your research question, you should be ready to locate a combination of primary and secondary sources relevant to your topic.

First, you should familiarize yourself with what constitutes a primary and a secondary source in your chosen subject.

You should also bear in mind that certain Extended Essays have a minimum expectation when it comes to primary and secondary sourcing, while others may disallow the use one type (for example, primary research in Psychology).

Subject-specific source lists

A tick (✓) indicates that the subject requires the use of that type of source, a cross (✗) indicates that it should not be included while a circle (o) indicates that it is dependent on the nature of the question devised. In most cases, the nature of the question dictates the type of sources required and thus it may be the case that both primary and secondary sources are required. Notes have been added to provide additional clarity on the requirements either way.

Subjects	Primary	Secondary	Notes
Language A	✓	o	The analysis should largely be based on the primary sources (that is, the text(s) being written about) from which all supporting information can come. Secondary sources can be used provided they are treated critically rather than merely accepted as the definitive interpretation.
Language B Category 1: Language Category 2: Culture and Society Category 3: Literature	 ✓ ✓ ✓	 ✓ ✓ o	With essays based on language or culture and society there is an expectation that reference to both primary and secondary sources should be made. With literature-based essays, the same rules as in language A apply.
Biology a. Experiment-based essay b. Non-experiment-based essay	 ✓ o	 ✓ ✓	**a.** The focus with experiment-based essays is the primary data produced as a result of the experiment(s) conducted by the student. Secondary sources in the form of scientific publications should be used to support a line of argument or indicate where the student has adapted their approach so as to produce different results. A consideration of the quality of the secondary source material should also be offered to identify limitations or weaknesses in approach, method and so forth. Note: There are restrictions placed on the use of animals and humans when it comes to experiment-based essays. For more, please check the IB's Animal Experimentation Policy with your supervisor. **b.** Non-experiment-based (literature) essays should effectively question the reliability of the secondary source material used, and offer some critical insight into the strengths and limitations of the methodological approaches taken by the secondary sources.

Subject			Notes
Business management	o	✓	Essays in business management can rest on secondary source material entirely. Where primary research is used, it must provide quantitative and qualitative analysis directly relevant to the question.
Chemistry **a.** Experiment-based essay **b.** Non-experiment-based essay	 ✓ o	 ✓ ✓	See biology notes.
Classical Greek and Latin	✓	✓	Students should aim to reference both types of source material. The text(s) studied will act as the primary source, while articles, reviews or other publications will constitute the secondary source material.
Computer Science	o	✓	Essays in computer science can be based on secondary source material entirely. A large number of such sources should be used where possible with the proviso that the most up-to-date material is found in every instance. Primary source material, in the form of programme runs or statistical charts, can also be used provided they are reliably constructed and relevant to the question.
Dance	✓	✓	Dance essays lean heavily towards primary source material (for example, interviews of dance practitioners or student's own dance experiences). Secondary source material (for example, texts about dance) should be used only as evidential support of your own perspective or argument. Challenging the position of a secondary source is also encouraged.
Design technology	✓	o	Due to the practical nature of this subject, most essays will focus on the design, implementation, benefits and effectiveness of your chosen product(s). A common approach would be to include data in the form of statistical charts, diagrams or tables gathered from user surveys and/or interviews of the product in action. More commonly, the sources used will often include your own data gathered from the trialling of a material, product or specific design, its experimentation for effectiveness, resilience or user-friendliness and so on or the production of models. Primary experimentation, however, is not a mandatory requirement although it does tend to lead to significantly better essays in design technology.

Subject	Primary	Secondary	Notes
Economics a. Research-based b. Source-based	✓ o	o ✓	Source requirements for economics essays are highly dependent on the nature of the question. Questions that invite and are dependent upon you conducting primary research (for example, interviews, surveys or questionnaires) are highly advisable though not mandatory. Essays based purely on secondary source materials (for example, economic data from the International Monetary Fund (IMF) and World Trade Organization (WTO)) are perfectly feasible provided the question has a sufficiently narrow scope. Essays that combine primary and secondary sources are also fine, provided both sets of sources are shown to be directly relevant to the question.
Environmental systems and societies (ESS) a. Experiment/Fieldwork-based b. Non-experiment/Fieldwork-based	✓ o	o ✓	Data gathered from experiments or fieldwork can constitute the entire basis for a successful essay in ESS, provided that detailed descriptions of the procedures used are given so that the work can be repeated independently. Essays based solely on secondary source material are also feasible, provided that a wide range of sources are used and that consideration for the reliability (or lack thereof) of said sources is made in the body of the essay. Some indication of how the material was created or the experiments it rests upon must also be noted in the essay.
Film	✓	o	As with a language A essay (see above), the primary focus of a film essay should be the primary source itself (that is, the film). Secondary sources can be used to support your line of argument but should not replace it. Secondary sources may also be challenged in the essay, rather than simply accepted as the definitive interpretation.
Geography	o	✓	Successful geography essays can be based solely on published secondary source material, however, a wide range of such sources would be required in this instance. Primary source work (for example, fieldwork data and questionnaires), although not mandatory, is highly advisable as it tends to produce stronger essays in this subject and thus yield higher results. In both cases, a critical evaluation of the sources/approach followed is required.
Global politics	o	✓	Essays in global politics require you to situate your question within existing theories or arguments related to the subject. As such, references to secondary source materials (for example, textbooks and books on ethics) are mandatory. The use of primary source material (for example, interviews and surveys), although not mandatory, is highly advised as it tends to result in a stronger essay and thus the potential for higher marks.

27

History	o	✓	Essays in history should aim to use both primary and secondary sources, although the IB recognizes that this may not always be possible with certain topics and thus is not mandatory. However, if primary source material is readily available, Extended Essays in history are expected to make reference to them. A primary source in history is deemed to be any artefact from the time in question, while a secondary source is anything written about that time but produced later. A critical analysis of the value and limitations of the sources used (both primary and secondary) by means of investigating their origin and purpose is also required. Factual data and historians' views should be used to support the students' own argument without replacing it.
Information technology in a global society (ITGS)	✓	✓	ITGS essays require the use of a wide range of both primary and secondary sources. What's more, an attempt should be made to support (or contest) findings in secondary source material with primary source work (for example, interviews and surveys). The selection of source material (that is, the approach the essay takes) should also be briefly and critically assessed in the body of the essay.
Literature and performance	✓	✓	Due to the interdisciplinary nature of the subject, any Extended Essay in literature and performance will require a thorough understanding of the primary text(s) studied and the context in which they have been "transformed" from one medium (text) to another (performance). This means that although the primary focus is the text itself (as with language A essays), the key difference here is that a comprehensive understanding of the pre-existing historical and cultural context is required in order to better evaluate the "transformation" (text to performance) aspect. As such, secondary source material (for example, literary critiques and critical evaluations) are required as part of any literature and performance essay. This can be supplemented with personal analyses of performances seen in galleries, cinemas, theatres and other performance spaces by the student.
Mathematics	✓	o	Essays in mathematics can rely solely on the analyses of the data produced by your own calculations or applications of the mathematical formulae associated with the differing mathematical disciplines. Secondary source material can be utilized if the focus of the question demands considerations of external proofs or approaches (for example, the application of a historical mathematical theorem on a contemporary school of mathematics).

Music	✓	✓	Music essays must analyse the primary source first and foremost (for example, performances and scores), however, secondary sources should also be used to provide support to the points raised by the student in the body of their essay. Where secondary sources are used, they must be used to support your own line of argument and not act as a substitute for it. An awareness of the value and limitations of the primary source(s) used is also required.
Peace and conflict studies	o	✓	It is a mandatory requirement that essays in this subject refer to at least one text that describes theories underpinning peace and conflict. There is a list of texts contained within the subject guide for peace and conflict studies that will be very useful for this aspect (speak to your IB Coordinator). Primary source material can also be used (such as interviews and surveys) where appropriate. This will become mandatory when there is not much secondary source material in existence on the chosen topic (for example, a conflict within a local community or school).
Philosophy	✓	✓	Primary sources in philosophy include the works of the philosophers themselves (e.g. Michel Foucault's *The Order of Things*) whereas secondary sources would include all other texts written about these works (including textbooks, articles, books and encyclopedias). Essays in philosophy should always begin with the primary sources while making use of secondary source material to further support a line of argument or analysis. Reliance on textbooks alone will produce poor philosophy essays and should be avoided.
Physics a. Experiment-based essay b. Non-experiment-based essay	 ✓ o	 ✓ ✓	See biology notes.
Politics	o	✓	Secondary sources (books about political theory) are a mandatory requirement for essays in politics. The student is expected to situate their question within relevant and existing theories of politics. Primary sources (for example, interviews and surveys) can be of use when the chosen topic is local in nature (for instance, an electoral process in a local community) but will still need to be grounded in established political theory (for instance, by showing an understanding of the democratic process).

Psychology	✗	✓	Psychology Extended Essays are expected to be seen as analytical investigations into an area of interest rather than primary research to test a hypothesis. Under **no** circumstances are students to engage in their own experiments or case studies as this is deemed inappropriate for essays in psychology. Instead, students should reference secondary source material as a minimum expectation (such as journals and textbooks) while making reference to pre-existing research material (for example, case studies and experiment-based data by recognized psychologists or institutions) as appropriate.
Social and cultural anthropology	o	✓	There is an expectation that all essays in this subject are rooted in a good understanding of anthropological theories and/or concepts. As such, reference to works by accepted anthropologists is highly advised. Primary source material can be included but must not be the core focus of the essay. A consideration of the value and limitations of the methodological approach followed to generate the data is also expected if primary source material is used.
Sports, exercise and health science **a.** Experiment-based essay **b.** Non-experiment-based essay	 ✓ o	 ✓ ✓	See Biology notes.
Theatre	✓	✓	Theatre Extended Essays require the use of both primary (the works themselves, artists, performances and so forth) and secondary sources (articles, books, journals and so on). You may also make use of their own primary data generated from interviews with theatre practitioners or visits to theatres and galleries or even the student's own experiences of performances.
Visual arts	✓	✓	Visual Arts Extended Essays must analyse the primary source(s) first and foremost (such as art and artists), however secondary sources should also be used to provide support to the points raised in the body of their essay. Where secondary sources are used, they must be used to support your own line of argument and not act as a substitute for it.
World religions	✓	✓	Essays in world religions work best when they evaluate the established approaches to religion as they appear in secondary sources (for example, works about religion) against the data collected from primary sources (for example, the sacred texts, interviews with religious figures or a community of believers). In both cases, sources should not automatically be treated as representative or authoritative.

World studies	✓	✓	World studies is unique in that it requires students to combine two subject methodologies (for example, history and visual arts). As such, the type of sources referenced will depend on the two chosen subjects. Refer to the specific subject information listed above for additional insight.

Types of sources

Accepted primary and secondary sources differ slightly in each subject, however, the table below will give you some indication of these.

Subjects	Primary sources	Secondary sources
Language A	Novels (text or graphic), letters, anthologies, poems, interviews, plays	– Any journals, articles, critiques, documentaries, websites, literary reviews, newspapers or literary magazines concerned with the chosen essay topic or its background. – Autobiographies and biographies may also prove useful in terms of context and occasional insight into textual meaning, although students should avoid limiting their analysis of the text to the specifics of an author's life
Language B	Novels, letters, poems, non-fiction, interviews, newspapers (language), websites (language), idiolects and dialects (language or culture), advertisements	Journals, articles, critiques, documentaries, websites, literary reviews, newspapers, literary magazines or any text focusing on language-specific analysis
Biology	Observations, fieldwork, experiments and all data generated from them	– Journals, articles, reviews, documentaries, websites, textbooks, science magazines on theories, experiments, models, case studies, approaches, research or methodologies – Data charts or graphs from science institutes or government centres
Business management	Any data, graphs, charts, position maps, matrixes produced by the student from conducting surveys, questionnaires, strengths, weaknesses, opportunities and threats (SWOT) analyses and any other acceptable quantitative or qualitative method as outlined by the business management syllabus	– Books, textbooks, articles, journal publications and websites on business theory, management or practice – Company reports, statistical bulletins or corporate analyses

Chemistry	Observations and experiments and all data generated from them	– Journals, articles, reviews, documentaries, websites, textbooks, science magazines on theories, experiments, models, case studies, approaches, research or methodologies – Data charts or graphs from science institutes or government centres
Classical Greek and Latin	Classical Greek or Latin texts such as epic poems, histories, speeches, political treatise, law codes and inscriptions	– Any journals, articles, critiques, documentaries, websites, literary reviews, newspapers, literary magazines and similar about the Classical Greek or Latin texts chosen for the essay
Computer science	– Analyses of student-made source code, compiler or other computer programme can form the basis of a computer science Extended Essay – Interviews with computer science experts (interviews of a small number of the student's peers would not be sufficient and should be avoided)	– Any specialist books, textbooks newspapers, magazines, journal articles and websites that reference the chosen computing system, programme, code, technology, hardware design and so forth
Dance	Dance productions (live or recorded), photos of dance performances, articles by dance practitioners or interviews with them, dance notations, student participation in performances or workshops related to their topic	– Any textbooks, journals, articles, critiques, documentaries, websites, dance reviews, dance magazines, promotional material or DVDs concerned with the chosen essay topic or its background
Design Technology	– Surveys, questionnaires, user observations and structured interviews with users and experts. – Any data in the form of graphs, tables, charts and so on that emerges out of practical experiment conducted by you (the user) could also feature although this is not mandatory. These experiments could take the form of performance and effectiveness tests, prototyping solutions, situation modelling, and design trialling.	– Books, textbooks, newspaper and magazine articles, journal publications and websites on design theory, principles, trends, applications and approaches – The usage of websites and textbooks alone is not sufficient for the purposes of an Extended Essay in design technology

Economics	Any data, graphs, charts and similar produced by the student from conducting surveys, questionnaires or interviews with experts in the field of economics (journalists, university professors, business leaders, politicians and other policy makers)	– Books, textbooks, newspaper and magazine articles, journals, and governmental publications and websites on economic theory, research, trends or policy – Research conducted by think tanks such as the Institute of Economic Affairs (IEA), Centre for Economic Policy Research (CEPR), RAND Corporation or similar – Publications produced by international organizations such as the United Nations, World Bank, International Monetary Fund and Golf Cooperation Council
Environmental systems and societies (ESS)	Observations, fieldwork, experiments, surveys or interviews with experts in the field of environmental studies	– Journals, articles, reviews, documentaries, websites, textbooks, magazines on theories, experiments, models, case studies, approaches, research or methodologies related to the environment, geography and biology could form the basis of secondary source material in ESS – Data charts or graphs from science institutes, government centres or international agencies (such as the Centre for Science and Environment, European Environment Agency and United Nations Environment Programme)
Film	– The film(s) or TV show(s) would act as the main primary source material, which would also include any scripts, screenplays, storyboards, and scores – Interviews with people involved in the film's production (whether via email or face-to-face) could also be used	– Any textbooks, journals, articles, critiques, documentaries, websites, film reviews, film magazines, promotional material or DVD special features/extras concerned with the chosen essay topic or its background

Geography	All data gathered from fieldwork investigations or studies (for example, sampling, questionnaires, interviews, surveys and mapping)	– Any books, textbooks, newspapers, magazines, journal articles and websites that reference geographical issues, approaches, research and methodologies – Aerial and satellite images – Digital landscape simulations and models – Diagrams, charts, reports and other statistical data obtained from reputable sources (for example, governmental agencies and independent environment organizations)
Global politics	Questionnaires, surveys and interviews with either experts in the topic under investigation (for example, university professors and government agencies) and/or stakeholders related to the political issues being investigated (such as policy makers, members of the community or family members)	– Any books, textbooks, newspapers, magazines, journal articles and websites that reference the chosen political issues, conceptual frameworks, research and approaches followed – Written or oral records of major stakeholders or participants
History	Texts or artifacts created at the time in question: such as histories, letters, images, objects, speeches, charters, laws, inscriptions, diaries, buildings, newspapers, posters and photos	– Texts concerning the time in question but created after it: histories, documentaries, websites, journals, history magazines and films
Information Technology in a Global Society (ITGS)	Any data gathered by the student through the application of ITGS theory, tools, and techniques (e.g. testing of a particular IT system's effectiveness, surveys on a system's usefulness or application, questionnaires relating to a system's usage, etc).	– Any specialist books, textbooks, newspapers, magazines, journal articles and websites that reference the chosen IT system(s) or overall IT-related concepts and applications in real-world scenarios. – IT think tanks such as the Information Technology and Innovation Foundation (ITIF) and similar

Literature and performance	– The focus here is on how a literary work (such as a novel, poem or short story was adapted into a performance (dance, play, opera, video game or film) – As such, the main primary sources will be the literary texts chosen and their associated adaptation – See the sections on language A, theatre, music, dance and so on for a list of relevant sources	– Any journals, articles, critiques, documentaries, websites, literary reviews, newspapers or literary magazines concerned with the chosen essay topic or its background – Autobiographies and biographies may also prove useful in terms of context and occasional insight into textual meaning, although students should avoid limiting their analysis of the text to the specifics of an author's life
Mathematics	– Axioms, proofs, equations, theorems, data, problems, conundrums, statistics and so on	– Books, journal articles, mathematics magazines, essays, specialist websites and any publication that incorporates mathematical techniques
Music	Music recordings, scores, performances, concerts, observations, workshops, interviews with performers, questionnaires and/or surveys	– Any textbooks, journals, articles, critiques, documentaries, websites, music reviews, music magazines, evaluations concerned with the chosen essay topic or its background
Philosophy	The original works of philosophers that outline their philosophical concepts or themes	– Any philosophy-related compendiums, dictionaries, textbooks and encyclopaedias – Where non-philosophy sources are used (for example, newspaper articles or literature on specific issues) they must be examined from a philosophical perspective only
Physics	Observations, experiments and all data generated from them	– Journals, articles, reviews, documentaries, websites, textbooks, science magazines on theories, experiments, models, case studies, approaches, research or methodologies – Data charts or graphs from science institutes or government centres
Psychology	Experiments, case studies, observations and similar would classify as primary sources in psychology, however, these are **not** permitted as part of the Extended Essay so students should not conduct primary research at all	– Books, journals, articles, reviews, documentaries, websites, textbooks, psychology magazines on theories, experiments, models, case studies, approaches, research or methodologies

Social and cultural anthropology	Observation, ethnographies, questionnaires and interviews (for example, life histories)	— Ethnographical and anthropological publications/studies will form the core source materials. Considerations of the ethical issues that underpin these studies is also necessary — Texts referencing social, cultural, political and historical contexts can be used for establishing wider contexts — Anthropology research libraries and institutes (for example, the British Museum's Anthropology Library and Wesley Powell Library of Anthropology)
Sports, exercise and health science	Observations, fieldwork, experiments, surveys or questionnaires, and all data generated from them	— Sports, exercise and health related books, journals, articles, reviews, documentaries, websites, textbooks, magazines on theories, experiments, models, case studies, approaches, research or methodologies in this area — Data charts or graphs from sports science institutes or government centres
Theatre	— The play itself (script/text or recorded performance) — Stage sketches, drawings, pictures, plans or photographs — Reviews of major productions — Interviews with playwrights, directors, actors, set designers, producers and so forth — Drama workshops	— Any textbooks, journals, articles, critiques, documentaries, websites, theatrical reviews, theatre magazines and evaluations concerned with the chosen essay topic or its background
Visual arts	The artwork and/or artist will constitute the main primary source material for Visual Arts Extended Essays — Exhibitions — Interviews with artists (via correspondence or face-to-face)	— Any textbooks, journals, articles, critiques, documentaries, websites, art reviews, art magazines and evaluations concerned with the chosen essay topic or its background
World religions	— Observation of religious practices or spaces — Surveys, questionnaires and interviews of religious leaders, practitioners or community members	— Religious/Sacred texts, images and artifacts — Any specialist books, treatises, newspapers, magazines, journal articles and websites that reference the chosen religious topic or theme — Written or oral records of major stakeholders or participants

World studies	A world studies essays requires that you select two subject areas to base your investigation upon. As such, the list of acceptable primary sources would depend on the chosen subjects See relevant subject areas above for lists of relevant sources	– A world studies essays requires that you select two subject areas to base your investigation upon. As such, the list of acceptable secondary sources would depend on the chosen subjects See relevant subject areas above for lists of relevant sources

Locating relevant sources

Most students gravitate to one of the main general search engines on the internet (for example, Google or Yahoo) or a general website such as Wikipedia as a first port-of-call when it comes to locating relevant sources. However, these do not always produce results that would be suitable for an academic research paper such as the Extended Essay.

Below is a list of alternative suggestions for a variety of subject areas:

Type	Details
1. Libraries	The **school's library** should be the first stop when it comes to locating relevant source material. Too often do students overlook their own facilities in preference of an electronic search engine much to the detriment of their final work. In addition to school libraries, many schools are within close proximity of **public municipal libraries** that often house significantly larger collections of materials. **State or national libraries** are also a great place to visit if they can be readily accessed. **University libraries** may also be available to you though borrowing restrictions may apply to non-university students. **Virtual libraries:** Many libraries of institutions (such as the Getty Research Institute) now make their resources available in a virtual (online) environment that is often freely accessible or requires normal membership as is the case with physical libraries. Many libraries have sharing agreements with larger (parent/associated) libraries, which means that resources can be shipped between them upon request. They also have paid subscriptions to online databases which members can freely access. Always bear in mind that librarians are best placed to support students with regards to the location of appropriate academic materials, be they print or electronic in nature.

Tip

Always visit a library.

2. Electronic databases

There are many electronic databases (many of them free or requiring a small subscription fee) that you can make use of. These usually store hundreds to thousands of academic-grade journals and associated publications. Below is a list of some of the more popular ones (check whether your library already has a subscription to these):

International System for Agricultural Science and Technology (AGRIS) (http://agris.fao.org/agris-search/index.do)
A free database containing articles in multiple languages on issues pertaining to the environment, geography and natural sciences.

The arXiv (http://arxiv.org/)
A free online database with publications relating to physics, computer sciences, mathematics, finance and biology.

CQ Researcher (http://library.cqpress.com/cqresearcher/)
A subscription-based database of contemporary social and political issues written by professional journalists.

EconBiz (www.econbiz.de)
A free online database with full-text access to a multitude of economics-related publications.

EBSCO*Host* (www.ebscohost.com)
A vast subscription-based database of scholarly publications, magazines and articles on most subjects. Includes many of these as full texts.

ERIC Institute of Education Sciences (http://eric.ed.gov/)
Thousands of publications relevant to education, human and natural sciences, the arts, and many more, often with free access to full texts or links to host sites.

Google Scholar (https://scholar.google.com/)
A search engine with a specific focus on scholarly articles, often accessible as full-text versions.

JSTOR (www.jstor.org)
A large subscription-based database of scholarly publications, magazines and articles on most subjects. Includes many of these as full texts.

JURN (http://www.jurn.org/)
A search engine with a specific focus on free scholarly articles, accessible as full text versions.

US National Archives (www.archives.gov)
A huge database of primary and secondary sources mainly on US History. Includes links to other external databases such as Fold3.

National Bureau of Economic Research (www.nber.org)
An online database with full-text access to a multitude of economics-related publications.

POPLINE (www.popline.org)
An online database with links to articles (often free) relating to health and associated factors such as culture and society).

PubMed Central (www.ncbi.nlm.nih.gov/pmc)
Database with millions of full-text articles on a myriad of topics in the Natural Sciences.

	Questia (www.questia.com) A vast, subscription-based database of scholarly publications, magazines and articles on most subjects. Includes many of these as full texts. **Science Direct** (www.sciencedirect.com) A subscription-based database of publications relevant to mathematics, the human and natural sciences.
3. Online encyclopedias	**An** online encyclopaedia such as Wikipedia is usually the first place a student will turn to when it comes to research. Due to the lack of peer review on such sites and their open editorial nature, these **do not** often work well as sources for academic research papers. Although students continue to include these as sources in their bibliographies, Extended Essays should also reference more scholarly material. Essays that rely solely, or heavily, on online summative encyclopaedias will not score well. However, these types of sites are useful for: a. providing an initial overview and summary b. providing links to a range of relevant primary and secondary sources in their bibliography sections for further investigation.
4. Books	When it comes to books, it does not matter if you have a digital or physical copy for use; more important is the quality of the book itself. For example, a history book written by an amateur historian (such as an ex-serviceman) or hobbyist may not be as scholarly as one written by a recognized professor of history. Likewise, if the history is written by an economist or anthropologist, the approach may not always be ideal for your essay. It is thus more crucial to evaluate your choice of books against your specific focus, rather than assume it is of use simply because it is a printed book. **Note** Far too often students assume printed works are all of the same quality, which leads to missed marks when it comes to Criterion A: Focus and Method and Criterion C: Critical Thinking. See *Chapter 4: Research (pages 49–61)* for strategies on how to maximize your evaluation of chosen sources.
5. Textbooks	Similar to online encyclopaedias, **no** Extended Essay should rely exclusively (or heavily) on school textbooks. They are great for initial ideas and overviews of content, however, you should seek more scholarly materials to supplement them.
6. Journals	You should always seek out information from acknowledged journals in your chosen subject. Online databases such as those listed above are excellent for this, however, physical copies may also be present in many local or school libraries. Alternatively, journals can be individually purchased directly from publishers. Major universities usually have publishing houses affiliated with them that publish academic journals covering a range of subjects (such as Oxford University Press, Cambridge University Press, Harvard University Press and University of Queensland Press). Their websites will list available publications for purchase.

7. Magazines	There are numerous specialized magazines that cover a wide variety of topics across all subject areas. A school's (or local/regional) library is always a great source of these types of publications. Below is a brief list of some examples:

- *New Scientist*
- *History Today*
- *BBC History Magazine*
- *BBC Music*
- *Philosophy Now*
- *IB Review*
- *Biological Sciences*
- *Chemistry Review*
- *Physics Review*
- *Psychology Review*
- *Economic Review*

- *Business Review*
- *Geography Review*
- *Frieze Magazine* (Art and Culture)
- *Creative Review*
- *Artforum*
- *Chez Nous Magazine* (French)
- *JDE – Le Journal des enfants* (French)
- *The Economist*
- *National Geographic*
- *Asian Theatre Journal*

8. Audio-visual	Videos or sound recordings such as documentaries, interviews, sound clips, demonstrations, 3D models and the like are also a great source of information that can feature in an Extended Essay.
	It is important to bear in mind that these must be audited for their reliability just as you would a website or book. Aim to source material from credible and acknowledged sources rather than using anything available on YouTube or similar channels.

Organizing source material

Once you have accumulated your resources, the next key step is to organize them so that you'll have an easier time referencing material when writing your essay.

Reading a pile of books, magazines and journals usually feels like a large part of the research work and once this is done, there is a tendency to simply jump straight into the writing of the essay. However, this approach is flawed as no matter how good one's memory, details and specific information will be lost or conflated with other bits of information when the time comes to write the essay simply because of the sheer number of sources used.

How do we go from numerous works to a single essay?

As the Extended Essay is written over a period of time (usually spanning a good year, if not more) this can often be used to your advantage by means of organized **note-taking**. The strength in taking notes in an organized manner is that you will then have a quick reference point for when writing your essay.

Below are examples of ways you could structure your reading and notes so as to minimize time spent later on re-reading your sources and instead maximize the grades awarded for critical thinking and engagement.

Source	**Info**	**Headings**
Source type (such as book, website and journal)	Summary of key points, bullet points of themes, ideas, research and so on.	What information have you extracted from the source that relates to your topic/question?
Use Microsoft® Word's automatic referencing feature or use an approved style (there are free online bibliography makers you could use).	Include quotes, page numbers, new references/paths of investigation and so forth.	Highlight possible paragraph topic sentences/thesis statements for inclusion in the essay proper.

Example grid:

Research question: To what extent was Pope Urban II's speech at Clermont (1095 AD) and the launching of the Crusades an attempt to increase Papal power in Europe in the 11th century?		
Source	**Info (or notes)**	**Topic headings**
Book: Somerville, R. (2011). *Pope Urban II's Council of Piacenza (March 1–7, 1095)*. Oxford: Oxford University Press.	Bernold of Constance confirms the receipt of emissaries from the Byzantine Emperor Alexius I while Pope Urban was in Piacenza (pp.15–16). "The legates implored [all] to provide assistance for defense 'of the holy church'"(p.15). Pope was attempting to support Alexius so as to gain influence in Byzantine Empire.	– Political (showed leadership and vision) – Religious (support for co-religionist Emperor in East) – Religious (support for co-religionist Emperor in East)
Magazine: Phillips, J. 11 November 2009. "The call of the crusades". *History Today*. Vol. 59, number 11. Pp 12–15.	Urban's motivation is difficult to decipher with certainty as much hagiography surrounds accounts related to him.	– Reliability of Sources
Book: …	…	…

The first column includes:

✓ all the relevant bibliographical details.

These can be lifted straight into your essay.

The second column includes:

✓ quotes

✓ relevant details

✓ mini analyses

✓ quick facts.

This is the place to store all of your key notes or evidence from the source material you have read. It will make it much easier to locate useful quotes or facts if you organize your reading and note-taking in this fashion.

All of the information here can again be embedded directly into your essay, as needed.

The third column includes:

✓ headings

✓ possible chapter titles

✓ factors.

This is very useful for structuring possible chapters in the Extended Essay, or developing key theses in the main body of the essay. As you read, you will invariably come across key ideas, themes, factors and so forth that you can use to respond to your essay's title. Colour-coding (or highlighting) the headings is useful for when you want to find specific notes rather than having to read through all of them again. In the above examples, all political factors are highlighted in red, while all religious factors appear in blue and so on.

Organizing chapters or paragraphs

Before beginning to write the essay it may also help to map out what key factors you feel are most relevant to your question's answer or development.

Two approaches are suggested below to help plan and organize your writing: (a) Mind maps and (b) Progression charts.

A. Mind maps

Mind maps are great for jotting down all the associated factors linked to a topic. However, there should ideally be two phases to this:

1. Firstly, write down all associated factors that come to mind or have emerged out of your reading

For example:

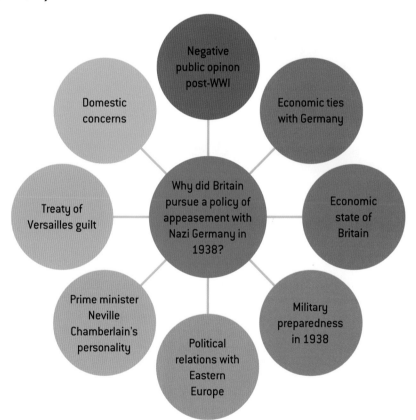

Neville Chamberlain was Prime minister of Britain from 1937 to 1940

2. Secondly, select the most pertinent factors for your specific essay. Sometimes, factors can be conflated into larger headings, which is always good practice. Remember, you do not have to include everything in order to successfully complete an Extended Essay. Sometimes removing factors from your list will help produce a sharper research question.

For example:

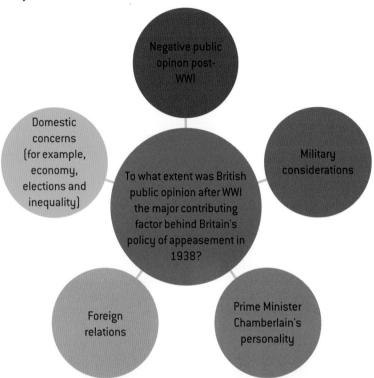

Top Tip

Having mind maps or progression charts like these as part of your Researcher's Reflection Space will come in very handy when trying to demonstrate engagement (Criterion E) with your chosen research topic.

B. Progression charts

With progression charts, you outline your key theses (or factors/points) that you believe fully respond to your research question. This allows you to visually plan how to write the essay and/or organize its sections into relevant chapters.

Thesis statement 1
Britain chose appeasement in 1937 due to the public outcry over the horrors of the First World War.
Possible chapter heading: Public opinion

Thesis statement 2
Britain chose appeasement due to concerns that its military forces were not adequately prepared for another conflict.
Possible chapter heading: Military preparedness

Thesis statement 3
Britain chose appeasement due to ongoing socio-economic problems.
Possible chapter heading: Socio-Economic Problems

C. Branches

Another way of organizing your chapters or paragraphs is by creating branches of associated factors or themes linked to a central area or topic.

In the example below, for instance, the first main chapter will focus on why Britain chose appeasement by exploring the role played by internal factors such as the problems facing the British economy and the negative public opinion following the First World War.

The point here is that you can keep extending a branch to cover all of the relevant factors while also considering other lines of inquiry in parallel.

RQ: To what extent was British public opinion after WWI the major contributing factor behind Britain's policy of appeasement in 1938?

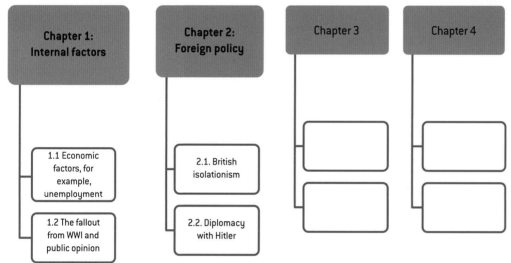

Evaluation

Value and limitations

It is vital, in all instances, that a consideration of the value and limitations of the selected research is offered. This will, more than anything, demonstrate a balanced and measured approach to data that is a requisite feature of all good academic writing.

Below is a list of statements that can be applied to a multitude of sources (both primary and secondary) when it comes to evaluating their value and limitations (or strengths and weaknesses). Do note, however, that some items listed as values may also be limitations and vice-versa. This is ultimately determined by the content or approach in question. For example, a questionnaire that relied on closed questions may not have produced the most reliable data when trying to determine motivations behind things like behaviour or justifications for action but could be seen as valuable in that it offered precise figures on people's reactions to specified stimuli.

Tip

Always consider the *value* and *limitations* of your chosen research method. Comment on this in the body of your essay.

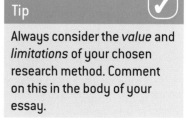

Values (strengths)	Limitations (weaknesses)
What makes a resource valuable (or useful)?	**What problems or weaknesses does the source indicate?**
• Its degree of objectivity (how factual it is in structure or approach)	• It contains bias (important to identify the nature of the bias and comment on its implications)
• It provides insight into thoughts or behaviours	• Purpose of source is to sway opinion
• Reveals weaknesses (for example, of a method, approach or historical figure)	• Its degree of subjectivity or one-sided perspective
• Provides accurate statistics or figures	• Contains hyperbole (exaggeration)
• Relies on a host of other sources	• Not written in the time in question (how many years removed is important sometimes as there could be issues with translation, and so forth)
• Contains quotes from key figures	
• Written during the period in question (eye-witness account?)	• Not written in place where events took place so access to information could be limited
• First-hand account of a party official or politician who had access to relevant information	• Lack of peer review or external moderation.
• Was not written under a censorship regime	• Proximity of author to figure in question (for example, a wife may be purposely misleading about her husband)
• Covers a wide period placing events in a wider context	
• Offers insight into personal views or opinions	• Political interference may mean author was not willing to express true sentiments
• Suggests motives for public actions and opinions	• Non-specialist (for example, an economist writing about politics)
• Indicates effects of an event or era on an individual	• Intention: Was it created for a specific audience (for example, humour or summary)?
• May indicate how the author (in the case of memoirs) wishes to be seen by public	• Is it a hagiographical (saintly) account of key figure?
• May offer an expert's view	
• May offer insight into emotional responses	• Could be a dissenting voice (thus offering an alternative interpretation)
• May suggest correlations between indicators (for example, unemployment and voting patterns)	• Cannot see beyond the lens or perspective intended by image maker (images)
• Can give a sense of a scene or event (images)	• May wish to highlight strengths of his/her actions
• Adheres to agreed methodological standards	• Offers only a partial understanding of topic
• Considers variables or anomalies	• Approach followed may be limited in scope
• Was peer reviewed or validated by multiple (recognized) external agents	• Based on leading questions
• Is free of bias	• Omitted variables or anomalies
• Produced a wide array of qualitative statements	• Produced a wide array of qualitative statements
• Contained closed or open questions (depends on what is being investigated)	• Contained closed or open questions (depends on what is being investigated)
• Could be applied to a multitude of cultures (that is, is not ethnocentric)	• Is ethnocentric and thus cannot be used to generalize across cultures
• Results in the source were standardized	• Results in the source were lacking in sufficient standardization

• Results were gathered in real-world and thus carry ecological validity	• Results were restricted to a lab and thus lack ecological validity.
• Methods used to produce results in the sources are not time-locked (that is, not applicable to current time frame)	• Results in sources may not be applicable to current time frame (that is, they're time-locked)

For example, if I chose to conduct a survey to ascertain whether student learning was enhanced by the use of a specific learning app, I should consider mentioning in my evaluation something along the lines of:

> *The survey results clearly indicate that student learning has indeed benefited from the use of App X, however, it is acknowledged that the survey's pre-coded and closed-question structure did not fully allow for qualitative statements to emerge that could be used to ascertain the specific degree to which learning was improved.*

What the highlighted section does is showcase my understanding of the issues associated with my chosen research approach while still enabling me to use the data/findings for the purposes of my analysis.

Grade Tip

As with any research tool used, it is useful to consider the advantages and disadvantages of the chosen approach as part of your analysis. Extended Essays that are aware of both the strengths and shortcomings of their chosen methodological approach achieve a higher score than those that do not. It is always good practice to indicate this awareness in the body of your essay or in the conclusion at the very least. See the advantages (strengths) and disadvantages (limitations) tables above for suggestions on what kinds of things could be included in your evaluation of methodology.

Evaluating methodology

When evaluating your chosen methodology consider including a section in your essay based upon your answers to the following questions:

a. How were your results achieved?	Explain how your data was collected or generated. This often includes a discussion of why you chose a particular methodology or list of secondary sources.

Example (ITGS):

Though the survey of my peers noted the preference for X app over its competitor, there is an acknowledgement that the sample may not have been large enough to more firmly ascertain if this preference is indeed widespread among smart phone users.

b. How was your data analysed?	Offer an explanation of any methodological problems and their solutions. You could also consider any effect that these problems may have had on your final results.

Example (Psychology):

The case study reveals that violent TV programmes do indeed elevate testosterone among young males, however, these results are largely ethnocentric in nature as the sample was only white Americans and thus may not be applicable to all cultures.

c. How reliable (or valid) was your chosen method or source material?	You should discuss the validity and reliability of the method used to generate your data as well as what steps have been taken to reduce any bias (or accommodate for it in secondary sources).

Example (History):

Although the ancient historian Herodotus' account provides us with seemingly exact figures with regards troop deployment, it must be acknowledged that he, like other contemporaries, was prone to exaggeration and hyperbole as that was the norm at the time. Thus his figures must be taken with a degree of skepticism and a lower number is more likely to be accurate.

d. Was there another approach that could (or needed to) have been followed?	You could acknowledge the limitations or issues with your chosen method by acknowledging the need or existence of an alternative approach which would yield a different conclusion.

Example (Business management):

The paper acknowledges that this evaluation is limited by its reliance on gross profit margin analysis which, though providing insight into Smartphone X's profitability after its introduction into the company's lineup of products, does not yield a big-picture overview of company growth (and profitability) as would be possible if a net profit margin analysis had been followed.

4: Research

In order to successfully respond to an Extended Essay's research question, a form of research must be carried out. For convenience, research can be divided into two types, primary and secondary:

a. Primary research (any data produced by you)

- Surveys
- Questionnaires
- Interviews
- Experiments
- Designs (and their testing)
- Models (and their testing)
- Measurements
- Field Studies

b. Secondary research (any analysis of pre-existing data by you)

- Literature review of secondary source material

Depending on the subject chosen, one form of research may be better suited than another; however, the key thing to bear in mind is that **a form** of research needs to be conducted. Even in Extended Essay subjects that have traditionally rested largely on personalised interpretations (for example, A essays) there is now a requirement that students engage in at least a literature review of sources pertaining to their topic so that they can better situate their own ideas within a wider body of discourse or debate.

> **Tip**
>
> No Extended Essay will score highly if simply based on opinion. The same applies if no acknowledged, subject-specific form of research is present.

The Extended Essay criteria now makes references such as the use of **"relevant"** sources (Criterion A) and that the writing needs to demonstrate a sound **"understanding and application"** of the chosen source material (Criterion B). As such, it is imperative that students include a form of research and subsequently make clear how it was utilised in developing their argument (see *Chapter 6: Assessment* for help with how to best demonstrate this so as to meet the criteria).

Research overview

Meaningful research usually follows a staged process that could be visually summed up as follows:

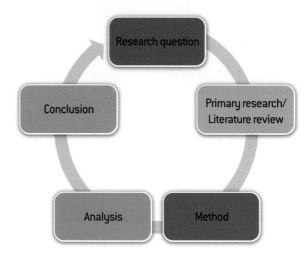

We generally begin with a question (or hypothesis), move on to a review of existing (and relevant) knowledge in our chosen field, decide upon a suitable method (or approach) with which to conduct our investigation, analyse the results or information gathered and finally arrive at a conclusion that, it is hoped, addresses our initial question.

The following sections will offer specific support for each of these research stages. You should also refer to *Chapter 3: Organising and evaluating* as it contains additional support for how to go about structuring and organising your work.

Research and the research question

In order to successfully conduct research one must first decide upon a question (or series of sub-questions) so as to give their research the necessary focus it requires. Reading "in general" around a topic does not yield as good a result as knowing exactly what it is you are trying to ascertain in the first place.

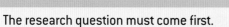

Note

The research question must come first.

The research question does not need to be definitive or final at the initial stage but some semblance of a focus is required in order to avoid wasting time sifting through material or conducting experiments that are not best suited to your investigation.

For example, trying to find research on "clean energy" for an environmental systems and societies essay will inevitably yield far too many results to be feasible for a student to read and analyse in the given 40 hours allocated to the completion of an Extended Essay. On the contrary, a student who has a more sharply focused question (for example, How effective are wind turbines at producing clean energy in the province of Galicia, Spain?) will be better suited at maximizing their time when it comes to the research aspect of their essay.

How effective are wind turbines at producing clean energy in the province of Galicia, Spain?

Primary research

This section is dedicated to various forms of primary research that a student may choose to engage in while also shedding some light on the core concepts of reliability, validity, value and limitations that every student engaged in research should be aware of.

Note

See *Chapter 2: Getting started* for more support with designing research questions.

Key issues and concepts in research

a. **Validity:** Data can be said to be valid if it provides an accurate picture of the reality it is referring to. When it comes to research, often one would seek either a total sample size or a random selection of a broad enough cross-section of that group.

> For example, if I am trying to determine how useful IB1 students find the Theory of Knowledge classes to their wider IB studies, I could:
>
> a. Survey the entire IB1 group.
>
> b. Place the names of all students in a hat and select a representative sample from it (say 50 for a group of 200 students).
>
> c. Allow a computer programme to generate a random list of 50 names that I could then survey.

All of these examples above would yield "valid" data pertaining to my research focus.

Why?

> Option A would be fully representative and provide the complete view; however, this may not work when the group in question is in the thousands or millions, or where time is not available to survey everyone.
>
> Options B and C work also as they provide a wide enough sample size from a random selection (thus eliminating any bias that would emerge if I interviewed say just one class who may have had bad experiences with TOK).

However, some research may not always accurately reflect the reality of the group being studied. For example, participants may not always respond truthfully to an interviewer's questions for various reasons (for example, they feel embarrassed or shy or they want to project a particular image).

For example:

Please don't snap!

In situations such as these, it is important to be aware that your approach may not always yield the most valid results and, where applicable, this should be acknowledged in the body of your essay (or in the conclusion at the very least).

b. **Reliability:** If you use the same method as a previous researcher, and get similarly consistent results, then the method you've used is considered "reliable". This may often mean repeating the exact same questionnaire used by another researcher with all members of the chosen sample, or relying on a method that many other experts in the field employ for similar investigations.

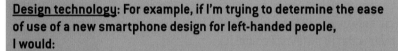

Design technology: For example, if I'm trying to determine the ease of use of a new smartphone design for left-handed people, I would:

a. Use a questionnaire similar (or identical) to one employed by other researchers on all users selected for my sample

Environmental systems and societies: If I'm trying to determine the evaporation rate of water in a nearby lake, I would:

b. Employ the equilibrium temperature method to measure the rate of water loss

Both of the above would produce "reliable" data.

Why?

Option A is reliable because the questions asked were exactly the same for all members of the sample and in line with other studies done on this topic. This would allow for some solid comparatives and considerations of any variables between the two (or more) surveys.

Option B is reliable because it employed a method that is used by experts in the field to measure the issue in question.

c. **Value and limitations**

It is vital, in all instances, that a consideration of the value and limitations of the selected research is offered as it, more than anything, demonstrates a balanced and measured approach to data that is a requisite feature of all good academic writing.

The evaluation of sources with regard to their value and limitations has already been covered in *Chapter 3: Organising and evaluating (see Evaluation on* pages 45–8 for more).

d. **Quantitative vs. qualitative**

There are two types of data that we usually end up with as a result of our primary research. Each have their advantages and disadvantages as shall become clear in the following pages.

Tip

Always consider the *value* and *limitations* of your chosen research method. Comment on this in the body of your essay.

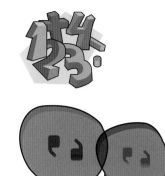

Quantitative data: Is information that is represented in number form or something that can be measured. For example, data on user preferences with regard to smartphone apps or distances achieved from use of varying parabolic curves can be represented as percentages, tables, bar charts and so on.

Qualitative data: Usually takes the form of descriptions or narratives that can reveal things such as people's feelings about a particular subject or event, people's emotional states or a wide array of opinions. For example, qualitative data can reveal what people think about a particular work of art or a recent governmental policy. This type of data is usually recorded in the form of words.

Methodology

a. Questionnaires

A questionnaire is a means of collecting information from a list of pre-set questions. It is a useful tool for conducting a social survey because it can be used to gather information from a large number of people. A survey can be a series of questions printed on a sheet of paper or completed online using one of the many online survey-making tools (for example, Survey Monkey, Zoomerang or SurveyGizmo).

Tip ✓
Always test your questionnaires with a small "pilot" group to see if your questions make sense to others, to correct any mistakes and to ascertain if you need to modify or include any further questions.

Closed questionnaires

In a closed questionnaire, the interviewee is asked a series of pre-set questions with a limited (or restricted) number of multiple-choice answers. For example:

Question and Answer
Question 1: How many hours do you spend on Facebook per day?

A. $0 \leq 1$	
B. $1 \leq 3$	
C. $4 \leq 6$	✓
D. $7 \leq 9$	
E. $10 \leq 12$	
F. $13+$	

Advantages	Disadvantages
● Produces easily quantifiable (measurable) results	● Limits possible choice of answers (no space for qualitative responses)
● Researcher controls the questions	● Imposition of questions on respondent may negate validity of research as it forces responses in a particular (pre-set) direction
● Produces reliable data that can be reproduced by others	● Closed questions cannot account for socio-cultural variances
● Quick response style means that sample can be quite large	● Researcher bias is increased due to limited (pre-set) responses
	● Responses may not be truthful

Open-ended questionnaires

In an open-ended questionnaire the interviewee is asked a series of pre-set questions for which they are able to dictate their own answers. For example:

Question and Answer

Question 1: What is your opinion of Facebook as a connectivity platform?

Well, I personally feel it is lacking ...

Advantages	Disadvantages
● Results tend to be more valid as respondents are able to more accurately comment on questions using their own words.	● Difficult to quantify these results by means of statistics or graphs as they are so varied.
● Responses tend to provide more detail and are thus qualitatively superior to closed questionnaires.	● May not be as reliable as closed questionnaires due to the wide range of possible responses.
● Responses not considered by the researcher may appear that could shed new light on the investigation being conducted.	● Quality and consistency of responses may not be high as respondents either ignore questions or provide answers that are difficult to interpret.
● Researcher bias is reduced due to openness of answers.	● Repetition of process may not be possible as it would likely yield differing results thus raising questions of reliability (or certainty) of data again.
	● Responses may not be truthful.

Questionnaires carried out by an interviewer

Interviews are often a useful way to generate research material. An interviewer must have pre-prepared a series of questions to ask, however, the interviewer can ask follow-up questions that arise from responses given. Respondents dictate their own answers to questions posed.

Advantages	Disadvantages
• Clarification can be sought in terms of responses given.	• Lack of confidentiality may eschew responses (interviewee may not be totally honest or may avoid giving a direct response).
• Additional, follow-up questions may arise based on responses, thus providing greater insight.	• Emotions may distort quality (and truthfulness) of response.
• Questions can be better explained to the respondent if required.	• Difficult to quantify results as they may be quite varied even if closed questions were used.
• Length of response could provide additional, qualitatively rich, data.	• Respondent could potentially be primed by interviewer's questioning.
	• Time factor involved may be significant.

b. Experiments

Experiments are a particularly strong means of ascertaining whether a research hypothesis is in fact valid and/or correct. Experiments are most often associated with Extended Essays taken in Group 4 subjects, although this does not mean that they are not possible in other areas such as geography or economics where experimental models can be developed and used to test hypotheses (for example, use of the Keynesian model of economic growth to ascertain the long-run aggregate supply curve or determining recession cycles based on the skyscraper theory).

Although there are a near infinite number of experiments one could conduct, certain basic rules apply to all of them. The checklist below should be referred to so as to ensure you are on the right track and do not fall foul of any experimental guidelines when setting up your experiment(s).

Note

You are **not** allowed to conduct experiments (or case studies) of your own for psychology Extended Essays.

Aspect	YES/NO
Pre-experiment	
1. Does your experiment meet the requirements listed in the IB ethical guidelines for Extended Essays?	
2. Does your experiment meet the requirements listed in the IB animal experimentation policy (if applicable)?	
3. Do you have all the necessary equipment to complete your experiment (checked availability with your school's relevant department)?	
4. Have you gained the required permissions to conduct your experiment (for example, from the science teacher, if using lab equipment in school; from the parks associations, if conducting research in a National Park; or from the government agency, if conducting experiments in public property)?	
5. Is the completion of the experiment feasible within the 40 hours outlined for the Extended Essay as a whole?	
6. Do you have all required safety equipment (and have taken the appropriate safety measures if using volatile elements)?	

Experiment	
7. Is the environment free of factors that could affect the experimental results?	
8. Have you prepared a chart or table where you will record your results?	
9. Have you isolated your (dependent and independent) variables?	
10. Have you incorporated a control into your experiment to act as a baseline?	
11. Have you repeated your experiment a number of times to guarantee the reliability of your results?	
Results	
12. Are your results free of researcher bias?	
13. Have you considered the possible limitations of your experimental approach (that is, would another method have yielded better/different results)?	
14. Have you considered what unanswered questions may yet remain?	

c. Literature-based methodological approaches

Research questions that do not lend themselves to primary research (such as are often seen in Extended Essays in literature, history and film) will invariably require a methodological approach that is rooted in secondary source material.

Below is a list of possible approaches to take when basing research on secondary source materials for a range of subjects. The table also includes examples of how to write about your approach in an introductory section of your Extended Essay:

Tip

It is highly recommended that you mention your chosen methodological approach in your introduction.

Subject	Methodological approach
Literature and languages	**1.** A close, personal reading of the texts (or language feature) in question For example: "This essay will offer a close, personal reading of both texts in order to determine Hemmingway's attitudes to religion in the works…" **2.** A close reading of a text (or language feature) based on a pre-existing literary theory or socio-cultural interpretation For example: "This essay seeks to determine the extent to which the characters in George RR Martin's *A Game of Thrones* challenge the "monomyth" hero archetype as outlined by Joseph Campbell…" **3.** A close reading of a text (or language feature) in order to either challenge or verify existing literary criticisms or critical responses For example: "This essay seeks to challenge the critical responses offered by Harold Bloom and Zadie Smith on the representations of love in…"

History	1. An analysis of an event or historical figure based on particular schools of history
	For example: "The orthodox interpretation blaming Nazi Germany and Imperial Japan for WWII will be evaluated in line with the arguments put forward by revisionist historians such as Taylor, Beard and Buchanan…"
	2. A comparative study of the historiographical traditions relating to an event or historical figure
	For example: "This essay evaluates the causes of the First Crusade by exploring the medieval historical accounts by Anna Komnena and William of Tyre and then counter-balancing them with those of more contemporary historians such as Asbridge and Runciman…"
Psychology* **Special note:** You are not permitted to conduct experiments as part of a Psychology Extended Essay therefore you are limited to a review of secondary source materials. * The same approach can be used with other group 3 (and even Group 4) subjects where a non-experimental approach is followed (for example, an essay in geography where no fieldwork is conducted).	1. A review of existing case studies
	For example: "This essay utilises the Koluchová twins (1976) and Genie (1977) case studies so as to determine the extent to which parental deprivation can lead to developmental delay in children…"
	2. An investigation based on existing experimental models (or approaches)
	For example: "This essay seeks to explore the nature of human obedience by investigating the results of both the Milgram and Asch experiments…"
	3. An investigation based on psychological theory
	For example: "By means of the developmental theories of Erikson and Kohlberg this essay seeks to evaluate the role played by the ego in shaping behaviour with a specific emphasis on motivation…"
Film* * The same approach can be used with other Group 6 subjects where a research question is purely based on secondary source material.	1. An evaluation based on an accepted film analysis approach, such as formalist, auteur, mythic and so on
	For example: "This essay employs a formalist analytical approach with a specific focus on how camera angles and special effects are used to enhance the theme of dread in Donnie Darko…"
	2. An analysis based on a socio-cultural or historical approach
	For example: "This essay explores the degree to which female characters in the TV series "Mad Men" challenge feminist film theorist Laura Mulvey's view that their role is largely to satisfy the scopic drive (viewing pleasure) of the audience…"

Mathematics	1. An analysis of the effectiveness or application of a given mathematical theory
	For example: "This essay utilises game theory (with a focus on probability) to determine the optimal approach a player of Blackjack would need to employ…"
	2. An exploration of the utility of mathematics (theory or models) in other disciplines
	For example: "This essay seeks to explore the reliability of inverse modelling when trying to ascertain optimal crop distribution in geography…"

Ethical considerations

Ethical issues and concepts in research:

- When carrying out research, it is very important to consider:
  - **Informed consent:** You should, as a matter of course, tell participants what they are doing and why they are doing it.
  - **How you report your findings:** You should always record and report your findings accurately and honestly.
  - **Harm:** Your research should always consider the physical, social and mental well-being of your participants and they should not be harmed by the research conducted.
  - **Anonymity:** You should, as a matter of course, change the name of participants in order to protect their privacy.

Literature review

What is it?

Despite what the title here suggests, a literature review is **not** a personal evaluation of works of literature such as those of Jane Austen or William Faulkner.

Literature here means *any collection of secondary sources or works produced on a given topic* (for example, journals, pamphlets, new articles and books). As such, it is relevant to **all** subject areas.

Definition: A literature review is a summative evaluation of what has already been written (or said) about a given topic.

What is its purpose?

Before writing about any topic (for example, the theme of justice in the works of Harper Lee, or the role played by nurture in the development of violent behaviour) it is useful to find out what has already been said about the topic.

This allows you to:

a. better understand the topic

b. make links between your ideas (or methods) and those of others

c. consider whether your ideas challenge or support an existing consensus

d. situate your views within a context of existing viewpoints

e. track any major trends or patterns in terms of interpretation

f. allow you to identify the value and limitations of source material.

Why do I need it?

No successful research paper such as an Extended Essay is written without basing its viewpoints on pre-existing literature. As such, a literature review forms the foundation and support for the development of your own voice, insight and contributions to the discussion.

How do I go about this?

When conducting a literature review we are usually trying to ascertain the following things:

Interpretations	Methodology	Results
• Identify what interpretations exist and if there are any patterns emerging among them. • Identify alternative justifications or judgements.	• Identify what approaches are best suited or recommended for your chosen topic/area of study. • Identify alternative methodological approaches to your topic/area of study.	• Determine which approach or sources are more reliable. • Identify any biases that may have affected the end results.

The following questions should help you conduct a literature review of your chosen sources:

Area	Question
Arguments	What are the main arguments or interpretations to emerge from the literature?
Themes	What are the main themes or areas covered by the literature reviewed?
Sections	What sections (or headings) can I sub-divide my topic into?

Problems	What are the key problems relating to my topic that emerge out of the review that I need to address?
	....
	....
	....
	....
	....
Consensus	What consensus of opinion or comparisons between sources exists?
	....
	....
	....
	....
	....
Contrast	What contrasting opinions exist within the literature reviewed?
	....
	....
	....
	....
	....
Method	How can the chosen theory or model be applied to your investigation?
	....
	....
	....
	....
	....
Limitations	What limitations can be identified in the method chosen or sources selected?
	....
	....
	....
	....
	....

Note

For support and recommendations on how to best go about structuring the analysis/conclusions of your literature review findings see *Chapter 3: Locating, organising and evaluating* (pp. 25–37).

How many sources are enough?

There is no right answer to this question. However, for the purposes of pre-university research a safe bet would be to aim for 5–10 quality sources, although this will obviously vary depending on the nature of the research question and topic chosen.

Tip

Aim for 5–10 quality sources when conducting a literature review.

Conclusions (research findings)

When examining your research findings or sources it is vital that you try to determine the following:

QUESTION:	ANSWER:
1. What "solution(s)" has your research indicated?	
2. What has been learned from the results or data?	
3. Were there any apparent contradictions that your research indicated? How have you accounted for these?	
4. What, if any, were the limitations of the research approach or methodology chosen?	
5. Are there any unanswered questions? Do they fall within the remit of your research question? If yes, how are you planning to answer them?	

5: Writing essays

When it comes to writing an essay there is no one approach that all students should follow in terms of both style and structure. This is even more the case when considering the myriad of subjects one can write an Extended Essay in, each with its own agreed upon approaches. For example, an essay in a natural science may benefit from more sub-headings or chapters while a literature essay may be more suited to a free-flowing approach.

Having said that, however, when writing a formal essay a minimum expectation exists that generally adheres to the following core model:

For the purposes of the Extended Essay, there are slightly different expectations to those that students are generally accustomed to when writing these three sections. The following pages are dedicated to helping students navigate these expectations while also providing some exemplar models that can be used to help structure their work.

Introduction

An introduction for an Extended Essay requires students to include the following aspects:

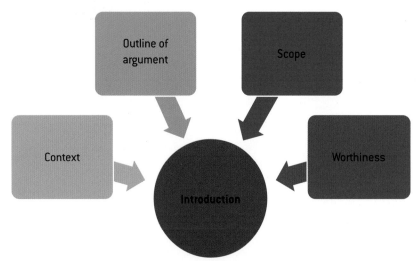

Aside from giving the essay a structural outline that any reader can follow, these aspects also help ensure that the expectations for Criterion A (Focus and Method) are met.

i. Context: Explicitly stating your research question and providing some context that situates your question within existing knowledge is key to a strong introduction. This does **not** mean providing detailed background information but rather indicating to an examiner what existing theories, critical approaches, methods or factors have already been suggested or exist to answer your research question.

ii. Outline of argument: Including the research question in your introduction is a quick way of ensuring you've made what you will be focusing on clear. In addition to this, it allows you to specify which aspects, factors or key features you will be investigating that will help answer your overall question. Doing this in the order they appear in the main body is advised.

> **Note**
>
> The Introduction in an Extended Essay is **not** the place to include detailed background information on an author, theory or topic. If you must include background information, save it for the main body or a separate section entitled "Background".

> **Tip** ✓
>
> Therefore, the **writing of the introduction often comes last**.

iii. Scope: It is vital that you indicate in your introduction *how* you've gone about answering your research question. This means indicating to the examiner what source material has been used, or scientific methodologies followed or critical interpretations challenged and so on.

Stating that your essay utilized websites, books and journals is not as good as indicating exactly which authors, theories or methods have been used.

> **Tip** ✓
>
> Therefore, wherever possible, **be specific.**

iv. Worthiness: Finally, it is important to indicate why your research question is worthy of investigation. Using the phrase "this research question is worthy of investigation because ..." forces you to consider worthiness by default.

The following list gives some indication of what is considered grounds for worthiness of investigation and what is not.

Worthy of investigation because:

- The question has contemporary application (for example, environmental benefits)
- The issues the question explores are controversial in nature (that is, they generate debate and have differing opinions relating to them rather than being simply scandalous in nature)
- The conclusion to this question may shed light on other areas or issues
- The investigation challenges existing theories or viewpoints
- The investigation explores the validity or reliability of a chosen theory or approach
- The question has not been covered or investigated before
- The question relates to a core field of contemporary research
- The topic is important in a geo-political sense as it affects X and Y groups of people
- The conclusions arrived at will enable greater understanding of the topic
- The conclusions arrived at will clarify existing misconceptions

Avoid:

- Selecting an investigation simply because you like the topic
- Selecting an investigation simply because you have had a good teacher
- Selecting an investigation because you were instructed to do so
- Selecting a topic where the conclusions act as a springboard for preaching or one-dimensional arguments
- Making emotional appeals (for example, if only everyone did "X" the world would be a better place)

Exemplar introduction: Below are sections of an introduction that showcase how to go about including the four core aspects outlined in 5.1.

Research question (history): *To what extent does Muawiya owe his accession to the Caliphate in 661 AD to the weakness of his principal rival, Caliph Ali?*

| Context | Muawiya's accession to the caliphate is a hotly debated topic among historians with some, such as Kennedy, arguing that he owes his elevation to the weakness of opposition as reflected in the figure of Caliph Ali, while others, such as Shaban, arguing that his success owes itself in large measure to the tangible economic benefits that support for Muawiya provided the Arab tribes ... |

| Outline of argument | ...this essay seeks to challenge the orthodox interpretation offered by Kennedy and instead argue that Muawiya's success owes much to the changing socio-economic dynamics among Arab tribesmen within the newly formed Islamic Empire ... |

| Scope | ...the essay will also simultaneously explore what other factors, including the governorship of Syria, the conflict with Byzantium, the dwindling role of the Ansar, and the role of the Kharijites played in helping Muawiya take over the Caliphate while relying on the works of principal historians such as Kennedy, Shaban, Armstrong and Hawting. |

| Worthiness of investigation | ...this research question is worthy of investigation because Muawiya's rise to the caliphate marks a significant turning point in the development of the Islamic Empire during the seventh century and beyond. It established the tradition of dynastic and monarchic succession that would become commonplace in the ensuing centuries ... the role played by Caliph Ali in supplanting the Rashidun model with a dynastic model is of critical significance to this early medieval period as it created the conditions for the schism between Sunni and Shi'a practices ... |

Recommended word count (Introduction): 300–450 words

Main body

As previously mentioned, the main body of an Extended Essay can differ structurally depending on which subject (or topic even) has been chosen. When structuring an Extended Essay the first consideration for the main body is to choose between a free-flow writing style or a more compartmentalized one where the essay is subdivided into sections or chapters.

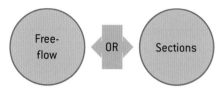

Although there is no hard and fast rule for this, the table below lists the most commonly seen approaches when it comes to structuring an essay in a particular subject (or topic area):

Subject/Topic	Approach
Literature	Free-flow
Language or culture	Sub-headings, chapters, free-flow
Humanities	Sub-headings, chapters
Sciences	Sub-headings, chapters
Mathematics	Sub-headings, chapters
Arts	Sub-headings, chapters, free-flow

Irrespective of the chosen approach, all essays benefit from some clear pre-planning with regards to the core points they wish to develop so as to answer their research question.

Identifying the essay's core points is of immense help when it comes to structuring your writing as it can form the basis of the sub-headings used (or in the case of a free-flow essay, the layout of the paragraphs) so that a developing argument is formed. (See Worksheet 2 on page 77 for more help with this.)

Paragraph writing

Irrespective of the approach selected, all essays should feature paragraphs. The important point to keep in mind when it comes to paragraphs is that they should indicate a shift from one line of argument to another, or from one developmental point to another.

The exemplar model below provides a structured approach to paragraph writing based on five parts that can be visually represented thus:

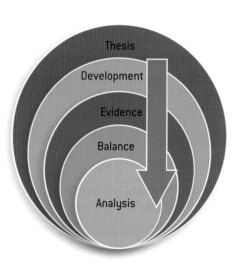

Thesis

- Thesis—a brief opening line (or two) establishing the key element to be covered in the paragraph.

Development

- **Development**—an elaboration of your principal thesis. The meaning of your thesis, the areas it touches upon and so forth.

- It should flow naturally from the thesis.

- It can offer mini-analyses as you wrestle with the implications of what you're saying.

Evidence

- **Evidence**—the most important part of each paragraph. All theses and points raised in your development should be supported by evidence.

  This could take the shape of:

- quotes from secondary sources

- examples from real-life situations (news, articles, events and so forth)

- examples and/or events from personal experience (the knower's perspective)

- facts and data (such as statistical information and measurements)

- illustrations and diagrams (both primary and secondary in nature).

Balance

- **Balance**—attempts should be made in either the existing paragraph or in a completely new one to offer alternative perspectives to the key thesis under consideration.

Analysis

- **Analysis**—at the end of each paragraph there should be a line (or two) linking the information back to the overall research question.

- Students should be able to answer the following question in each paragraph:

  What insight does this paragraph offer to the overall question?

- It could also suggest any contradictions/unresolved issues.

Exemplar paragraph: Below is a full example of how to use this five-stage model to structure your paragraphs.

Research question (history): *How significant a role did the Prophet Muhammad's military victories play to the rise of Islam in the Arabian Peninsula?*

The paragraph

1. Thesis statement (or topic sentence): Establishes what point or issue your paragraph is going to develop. This should be written in the form of a statement that is relevant to the overall question or topic being addressed.

For example: Muhammad's string of early military victories, primarily against the Quresh, were a significant factor in the early development of Islam.

2. Elaboration (development): Explains in greater detail what is meant by the thesis statement.

For example: During Muhammad's prolonged exile in Yathrib (Medina) from 622 to 630, his position as the pre-eminent religious leader of the nascent Islamic community (umma) was consolidated and secured by his abilities to defeat the enemies of Islam in accordance with practices the local Arabs (badw) would recognize as noteworthy. Muhammad, in true tribal chieftain form, was able to attract supporters to his fold through the pursuit of raids and campaigns which bolstered his reputation and standing among his fellow men.

3. Evidence, events, examples: All statements must be supported by one or more pieces of evidence.

For example: According to Armstrong, the Prophet Muhammad's victory at Badr "impressed the Bedouin tribes, some of whom enjoyed seeing ... the mighty Quraysh brought low" (Armstrong, 2001, p.17). In time, Muhammad's victory at the Battle of the Trench where his force of 3,000 defeated a force three times larger "convinced the nomadic tribes that Muhammad was the coming man and made the Quraysh look decidedly passé" (Armstrong, 2001, p.17).

4. Balance: Offer an argument opposite to the one you are making to show you have looked at the issue from more than one angle, but make sure you counter-argue so that you have still made your point.

> **Note**
>
> This could be its own paragraph in certain cases or it could be blended in to all paragraphs in the main body.

For example: However, despite the prestige gained from Muhammad's victories, these alone would have been worth nothing had he not followed it up with a more localized campaign in Medina and its surrounds to root out his most dangerous ideological rivals, principal among those being the Jewish clans who had aligned themselves with the Meccans (Qaynuqah, Nadir and Qurayzah). By crushing them, and in the case of the Qurayzah, massacring all 700 of their men and selling their women and children into slavery, he ensured that his military victories brought about more long-term benefits.

5. Analysis: The last few lines of your paragraph should answer the following question:

● What does all of the above have to do with the question?

OR

● How does the above information link back to the question?

For example: It becomes increasingly clear, therefore, that Muhammad's military victories significantly aided his reputation and prestige among the Arab tribes by playing on local sensitivities and traditions of "good" leadership. However, these would not have translated into long-term benefits had it not been for his parallel campaign against ideological and political rival bases.

—Armstrong, K., *A Short History of Islam*, 2002

Recommended word count (Conclusion): 350–450 words

1. Personal pronouns in sentences.

For example: "I believe/think that one of the factors that led to Muhammad's victories ..." Instead, frame the sentence into a statement:

For example: "One of the major factors that led to the rise of Islam in the sixth century ..."

2. Direct YES/NO responses in your introductions and conclusions.

For example: "No, I disagree that the military victories ..."

Instead, frame the response into a statement that establishes your viewpoint:

For example: "It is difficult to agree with the statement that the military campaigns alone ..."

3. Incorrect spelling of familiar or key words. Whether you like it or not consistent bad spelling of key terms and words creates a negative impression.

For example: "new York", "hitler" and "effect vs. affect".

4. Excessive narrative. Avoid writing a history of events. Examiners are looking for an analysis of events, not a full retelling.

For example: "... did play a part because that led to an argument between Muhammad and the Quresh which then led to a war where many people were killed ... and then there was a reprisal attack."

Instead, opt for a summative statement or major topic sentence/heading that includes all the information within it.

For example: "The military campaigns played a critical part in establishing Islam as the predominant socio-cultural force in Arabia and by extension a political power as it exploited the pre-existing Arabic cultural norms."

5. Inaccuracies.

For example: "The Battle of Waterloo was a military victory for the Napoleon."

Instead, ensure you revise your notes so that your content is 100% accurate.

6. Use punctuation marks.

Don't be scared of the full stop! When the central meaning of a sentence changes you need to indicate that with a full stop. Commas are also helpful to break up linked ideas within a long sentence.

Analysis

When conducting an analysis you are effectively relating the material gathered to the primary focus and objectives of your Extended Essay's research question. The key questions you should be asking of your sources are:

1. How does the information gathered relate to my question?

2. What answer (even partial) does the source provide?

When conducting an analysis:

- you must demonstrate a scholarly interpretation of your findings— this means that you must draw links to academic theories or approaches relevant to your subject, not simply tell a narrative or provide a description of the data

- you must provide evidence to support your various points and highlight the relationship between them. This often means referring to your primary and secondary research findings (including any statistics, tables and diagrams) to support your argument.

Remember

Remember, examiners want to see a logical argument develop that is well-supported by relevant evidence.

Analytical structure: How to demonstrate analysis in writing

The following tips and strategies are aimed at ensuring that your writing is structured in such a way that it ensures that analysis is taking place.

Signposts indicating critical discussion:		
1. Use reporting verbs	Reporting verbs help strengthen and support a line of argument while also indicating to the examiner why or how the source is useful. There is a near infinite amount of reporting verbs but some of the most common can be found below:	
i. verbs that present the author's viewpoint	Jeffery (1997) **argues** ...	Thurston (2001) **disputes** ...
	Henderson (2014) **conceded** ...	Birimac (2011) **reinforced** ...
ii. verbs that offer a neutral or objective assessment	Chittenden (1998) **describes** ...	Pagomenakis (2004) **states** ...
	Halstead (1992) **defines** ...	Jones (1999) **highlights** ...
iii. provide insight into the thoughts and feelings of the author	Santrampurwala (1999) **contested** ...	Mc Glinchey (2000) **evaluated** ...
	Mc Mullen (2010) **investigated** ...	Bell (1978) **estimated** ...
	Richardson (1996) **believes** ...	Rees (2003) **recognizes** ...
iv. other useful verbs	Analysed	Indicated
	Claimed	Noted
	Compared	Observed
	Commented	Pointed out
	Concluded	Reported
	Criticized	Showed
	Demonstrated	Suggested
	Discussed	Validated
	Illustrated	Verified

2. Skip a line	When writing, skip a line between paragraphs to indicate to an examiner that you are moving on to another analytical point.
3. Use linking words	In order to ensure your argument flows you must link your ideas together so they read as one developing argument. The best way to ensure this is by means of linking words.
i. when building up an argument	and, also, as well as, moreover, further, furthermore, in addition, additionally, next, secondly, thirdly, in conjunction
ii. when drawing comparisons	similarly, likewise, in the same way, equally, challenging
iii. when highlighting contrasts	although, for all that, however, on the contrary, conversely, otherwise, yet, but, even so, despite
iv. when indicating both similarities and/or differences	yet, even so, despite, notwithstanding
v. when providing reasons or a rationale	for this reason, to this end, for this purpose, because, since, so that
vi. when explaining results	as, as a consequence, as a result, hence, therefore, thus, inevitably, so
vii. when citing examples	for example, for instance, in other words, by way of illustration, such as, this demonstrates, which can be seen in, as cited by
viii. when arriving at conclusions	as has been noted, finally, in brief, in short, to summarize, consequently, therefore, in conclusion, in other words, accordingly
4. Create a logical order	Read through your work and then move the paragraphs or sections around so that the argument flows or develops in a logical order.
5. Use sources *All quotes below have been written by the author for demonstration purposes only.	Sources must always act as the bedrock of any analysis as they provide an externally validated support to your own ideas and writing. Sources should be used to ensure the following:
i. **provide further explanations.**	Use a source to add further detail to a line of argument or to some relevant facts you've referred to. *For example:* The Fourth Lateran Council provided Pope Innocent III with a platform to re-impose Papal authority over European bishops, which Geralt adds was also "a much needed stimulus for the Papacy".

ii. provide agreement.	Use a source to provide agreement or arrive at a consensus on a point or key issue.
	For example: The Fourth Lateran Council was a watershed moment for Pope Innocent III as it not only provided him with a basis for re-imposing papal authority over the bishops but also signalled the power of Papal institutions. This is a view shared by Merigold who argues that "Innocent's council marked the beginning of a return to form for the Papacy".
iii. provide alternative viewpoints or approaches.	Use a source to provide alternative points of view or varied approaches to a key point or issue.
	For example: The Fourth Lateran Council was a watershed moment for Pope Innocent III as it not only provided him with a basis for re-imposing papal authority over the bishops but also signalled the power of Papal institutions. However, Riannon argues that "Innocent's council marked a last ditch, desperate move by the Pope to regain the initiative".
6. Be heard	Provide your own voice to any discussion or debate by commenting on the results, data and any findings you've come by.
	Ask the ever important question: *What does this information reveal about my research question?*

Conclusion

The conclusion to an Extended Essay must be taken very seriously as it brings your essay to a formal close.

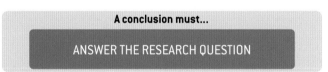

A conclusion must...

ANSWER THE RESEARCH QUESTION

The conclusion should reiterate the key findings and main points developed in the body of the essay and provide a resolution to your research question.

Below are a list of things that can feature in a conclusion and things to avoid at all costs.

Good:

1. A response to the actual question on your title page (ensure you have not drifted into responding to a slightly different question or focus).

2. Comment on any inconclusive findings or multiple interpretations if that is what your research has indicated.

3. Disprove your core thesis if your evidence has led you to this conclusion.

4. Offer an evaluation of the value and limitations of the methodology, process or sources you have utilized.

5. Mention any unresolved or additional questions that have arisen as a result of your research and why their answer goes beyond the remit of the current work.

6. Summarize the key points raised in the main body and synthesize them into a final analysis.

Avoid:

1. Introducing any new material (this includes quotes not seen before in the essay).

2. Offering no conclusion whatsoever (you should offer a resolution even if it is partial or incomplete).

3. Including any emotive or personal statements.

4. Including any accusations (it is not your role to judge).

5. Answering a question that is different to the one on the cover.

Exemplar paragraph: Below is an example showcasing a conclusion that meets the general requirements as outlined above.

Research question (English Literature): To what extent could Bram Stoker's *Dracula* be read as a representation of British imperial anxieties relating to reverse colonization?

Summarize main points

Stoker's Britain was a nation that had forged for itself a colonial empire. The English had invaded the "primitive" peoples of the globe and brought with them the "gifts" of their civilization. In Stoker's time, however, this imperialistic policy seems to have created a sentiment of fear and guilt, a sentiment that would be poignantly brought home in the figure of Dracula who acts as a potent figurehead of reverse colonization in action. This fear of reverse colonization, as has been made clear in the essay is coupled of course with a profound

sense of guilt at the situation of domination and subservience created out of Britain's imperialistic hegemony. The England of Stoker's time was in doubt as to her right to rule these "primitive" peoples and feared that one day the situation may be reversed. These fears and guilt were a natural by-product of the acknowledgment of the cycle of history that outlined how one race gave way to another, how one civilization replaced another and so on and so forth. It was now England's turn to feel the sting of history and to begin to question their empire's stability.

Offer summative synthesis of key points (linked to RQ)

Stoker, being acutely aware of this imperialistic crisis that gripped his country during the nineteenth century, expressed it quite potently in the figure of Dracula who seduces upstanding British citizens (Lucy, Mina and so on) through a combination of blood contamination and, more alarmingly to the Victorian mind frame, through his skillful mirroring and appropriation of 'civilized' British practices (legal contracts, seek advice from solicitors, land ownership, Victorian attire and so forth). ... Dracula's calculated invasion of England, therefore, could easily be read as the threat of reverse colonization coming out of the East. The end result is a character and novel that stands as a signature projection of contemporary anxieties transposed onto the pages of horror fiction.

Acknowledge limitations

Naturally, this essay acknowledges that this is only one of a myriad of possible interpretations and that the socio-historical approach followed here ignores possible psychological or genre-specific readings that may yet challenge the points raised within this essay.

Recommended word count (Conclusion): 350–450 words

Worksheet 1: Meeting the introduction requirements

1. CONTEXT: What key aspects can you discuss to ensure you've provided some context underpinning your research question?

2. OUTLINE OF ARGUMENT: What features, aspects, factors, theories and so forth will your essay utilize in order to arrive at a conclusion?

3. SCOPE: What authors, scientists, case studies, theories and so on have been consulted to answer your research question? *Remember to be specific.*

WORTHINESS: Why is your research question worthy of investigation?

Worksheet 2: Organizing the main body's key points

A. Identify the main points you are going to develop in the body of your essay that directly relate to your research question.

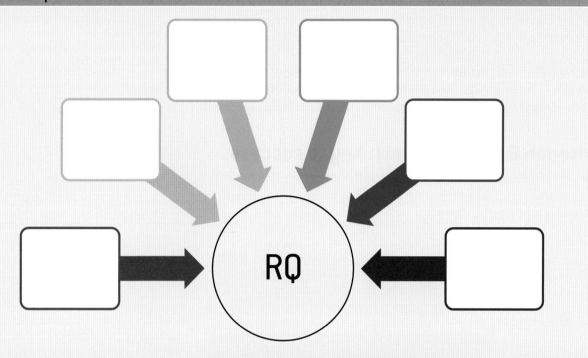

B. Now place them in the order that best enables an argument to develop. You may wish to start with your strongest point or a factor included in the research question itself before moving on to other subsidiary points (or factors).

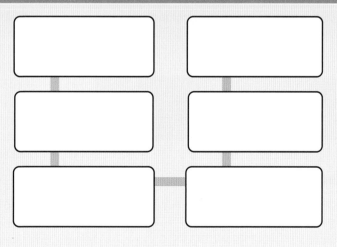

6: Supervision

This chapter focuses on the process of supervising an Extended Essay and therefore is aimed at supporting you (and your supervisor) with regards to maximizing the input and feedback from the supervisory sessions. This will include the three mandatory sessions that form the basis for completing the Reflections on Planning and Progress Form (RPPF) that is now submitted along with the Extended Essay itself.

Criterion E (Engagement): Key to success

The key to being awarded the six marks for Criterion E is for you to demonstrate engagement with the research process. This is achieved through commenting on:

 a. the thinking behind a chosen subject and eventual research question

 b. the methodology and/or selection of source material

 c. challenges encountered during the research process and solutions attempted or found

 d. creative or innovative approaches to the topic (and/or to the challenges encountered).

Exemplar calendar

Below is an exemplar calendar for the Extended Essay that is based on northern hemisphere school years (September–June), although could easily be adapted for southern hemisphere purposes.

The calendar outlines the types of support sessions a school's Extended Essay Coordinator (or IB Coordinator) and other support staff (such as librarians) could run for both students and staff to ensure consistency in terms of approach to Extended Essay guidelines and requisite skills.

Supervisory guidance

No Extended Essay is successful without adequate supervisory support, however, what is occasionally overlooked is that supervisors also require support, especially when it comes to structuring the supervisory sessions they will be having with their tutees. The following section aims to offer structural support for coordinators and, by extension, supervisors and students so that the most can be made of the planned sessions.

The EE calendar is punctuated at the end of the first year of your IB studies with a presentation showcase (called the EE Café) where you present your findings up to that point to a panel of "judges" who can evaluate if you are on track to begin writing your Extended Essay between the first year of your IB studies and the beginning of the second. An exemplar model for this event is included on page 80.

The calendar also includes Progress Check Forms, Contracts and Support Emails that an EE Coordinator could use to keep track of your progress, and support you and your supervisor throughout the duration of the Extended Essay process. Exemplars for all of these aspects can be found from page 82 onwards.

EXTENDED ESSAY CALENDAR			
Step/Timeframe	**Details**	**Forms/Due**	**Support**
CORE SKILLS September–October	• **Research methods** (Quantitative, Qualitative, Interviews, Online journals and so forth) • **Referencing skills** • **Literature review skills** • **Assessment criteria outlined**		EE Coordinator/Librarian sessions on these attributes
STEP 1 Early November	• **Generating research questions**		**Students:** EE Coordinator session on research questions **Staff:** EE Coordinator workshop on RQs
STEP 2 Late November	• **Feasibility / Viability report** (Students to submit 5–10 sources correctly referenced to prove viability of proposed RQ)	• **Form 1** • **Contract**	
STEP 3 Mid-December	• **Issuing of supervisory lists to students** • **Re-introduction to assessment criteria**		**Students:** Session by EE Coordinator on EE assessment criteria Distribution of criteria booklet **Staff:** Session on assessment criteria (subject-specific)
STEP 4 Early/Mid-January	• Schedule appointment with supervisor and meet for first time	• **Form 2**	**Staff:** Support email sent to staff with list of points to cover in first session. See page 86 on First Meeting for things to include.
STEP 5 Mid-January–Mid-March	• Meet with allocated supervisor at least two times (10–20 min sessions) • Complete first reflection (RPPF)	• **Form 3**	**Staff:** Support email sent to staff with list of things to cover in preparation for Form 3.

STEP 6 Mid-March–June	• Students prepare for Extended Essay Café (presentation). **EE Café summary** Students to present the following: 1. Research question 2. Background into topic chosen 3. Details from two proposed chapters of their EE (relevant to RQ) 4. Detailed bibliography (using approved style) 5. Problems encountered and solutions proposed 6. Plan for summer Meet with supervisor before this. • EE Café should ideally be a full-day of timetable. • Parents can be invited to this session.	• **Form 4** (can be completed on day of EE Café)	**Students:** Presentation to students outlining requirements and presenting exemplars by IB Team (and potential volunteer) **Staff:** Support email outlining EE Café process and recommendations for support during meetings with students
SUMMER June–September	• Students to begin writing first draft of their EE.		
STEP 7 (The second year of your IB studies) September–October	• Students to submit complete first draft, **including** Turnitin (or similar plagiarism) Report • Complete Second Reflection (RPPF)		**Students:** IB Team session on: 1. Presentation 2. Introduction 3. Conclusion **Staff:** Turnitin (or similar plagiarism check) workshop
Marking and feedback October	• Supervisors to read and provide feedback on submitted First Drafts		**Staff (optional):** Refresher workshop on assessment criteria
Moderation	• Departments to moderate EE (as required)		
STEP 8 October–December	• Students to work on their first drafts with aim to produce final version • Final version to be submitted	*Final version due:* December	

STEP 9 Viva voce	• Students to make appointment with supervisors so as to complete the viva voce (interview) • Complete third reflection (RPPF)		**Students:** IB Session on "viva voce"—What to expect and how to plan for it **Staff:** Support email with viva voce guiding question and exemplars

Supervisor guidance: Contract and progress forms

Many schools now opt to have their students sign an undertaking (or contract) that outlines the student's responsibilities and the nature of the supervisory support they will receive. Below is an exemplar contract that supervisors may consider using or adapting for their own purposes.

Bear in mind that the IB does not mandate such contracts, but they do prove useful as a means to familiarize students with their obligations when it comes to this independent research task while also making them aware of the limitations imposed by the IB on the support available.

Exemplar "Progress Forms" can be found on the following pages to help with the management of the Extended Essay for both the student and the supervisor/coordinator. These are divided in accordance with the exemplar assessment calendar above and are intended to help supervisors and coordinators monitor their tutee's Extended Essay progress.

Overview of forms

Form	Purpose
Student Undertaking	An exemplar form to be signed by you, the student, whereby you indicate your understanding of your obligations in relation to the Extended Essay and acknowledge the extent of your supervisor's role in the process.
Proposed Subject and Topic	An initial form that you can complete to indicate your choice of subject(s)/topic(s) that you wish to pursue for consideration by a coordinator/supervisor.
Research Readiness	This form is intended to document a student's completion of key preliminary steps before they begin the in-depth research and reading that will lead up to the initial writing phase.
Writing Readiness	This form is focused on documenting your readiness to begin writing the Extended Essay (or at least sections of it) after having completed an adequate amount of research.
Progress Check	This form should act as a summative snapshot of your progress (both in terms of research and initial writing) usually before the end of the first year of your IB studies. It works very well when you are expected to present your work "to date" to your supervisor in a format similar to the one suggested on page 80.

Student undertaking (Extended Essay)			
Student's name:		**Candidate number:**	
Supervisor:		**EE subject:**	

A. I hereby recognize that as a student undertaking an Extended Essay as part of my IB Diploma or Diploma courses it is my responsibility to:

- read the latest version of the general guidelines for the Extended Essay ☐
- read the subject-specific guidelines for my chosen Extended Essay subject ☐
- adhere to any deadlines and meeting requests specified by the EE Coordinator and my supervisor ☐
- adhere to all policies relating to academic honesty, especially with regards to the referencing of all source material used in my Extended Essay, and agree that any breaches with regards to academic honesty are my responsibility ☐
- adhere to the IB's ethical guidelines at all times. ☐

B. I hereby also acknowledge that my supervisor's responsibility is to:

- provide encouragement and advice specific to the subject/topic chosen ☐
- provide general guidance with regards to appropriate research skills ☐
- validate the originality of my work ☐
- provide me with one piece of formal feedback (on the first complete draft) ☐
- complete the supervisory report/sign my Reflections on Planning and Progress Form (RPPF). ☐

C. I hereby also acknowledge that my supervisor's responsibility is not to:

- tell me what to write or provide me with a research question ☐
- provide me with the research or source material ☐
- edit my work (including annotating writing and/or checking my research findings) ☐
- spend more than five hours (cumulatively) supervising my EE. ☐

D. I understand that my supervisor, although striving to support me in the best possible way, cannot guarantee a specific grade. ☐

E. Finally, I recognize and agree that no grade will be awarded for the Extended Essay if I am found in breach of the rules governing academic honesty. ☐

Student signature:		**Parental signature:**	
Date:		**Date:**	
Supervisor signature:		**Coordinator's signature:**	
Date:		**Date:**	

Extended Essay progress form	1
Proposed subject and topic	

Due by [   ] to the IBDP/EE Coordinator

Student name:

Diploma subject choices:	
Higher level	**Standard level**

Proposed EE subject (Choice 1)	
Specific topic area or initial research question	
Rationale for choosing this topic area	
Proposed EE subject (Choice 2)	
Specific topic area or initial research question	
Rationale for choosing this topic area	

Has the student attached a list of suitable sources (feasibility study) to support the proposed essay topics?	**Yes** ☐	**No** ☐	**Comments**

Student signature:		**Date:**	
Coordinator signature:		**Date:**	

Extended Essay progress form			2
Research readiness			

Due by [   ] to the IBDP/EE Coordinator

Student name:		Supervisor:	
Subject:			
Proposed research question:			

Research preparation check			
Action	**Yes**	**No**	**Supervisor's comments**
1. Has the student organized and attended planned meetings?	☐	☐	
2. Has the student been made aware of the general guidelines for the EE (for example, ethical guidelines)?	☐	☐	
3. Has the student been made aware of the general and subject-specific assessment criteria?	☐	☐	
4. Has the student prepared a bibliography of relevant source materials?	☐	☐	
5. Has the student engaged in any preliminary reading around their topic?	☐	☐	
6. Does the student have a refined research question?	☐	☐	
7. Does the student possess the necessary skills to conduct an EE in this subject?	☐	☐	
8. Is the student's attitude to the research process adequate?	☐	☐	

Additional comments			

Student signature:		Date:	
Supervisor's signature:		Date:	

Extended Essay progress form			3
Writing readiness			

Due by [   ] to the IBDP/EE Coordinator

Student name:		Supervisor:

Subject:

Refined research question: ....
....

Writing readiness check			
Action	Yes	No	Supervisor's comments
1. Can the student demonstrate completion of planned reading/research? This includes (as applicable): • experiments • fieldwork • writing of notes • data recording • organization and analysis of findings.	☐	☐	
2. Does the student intend (or need) to complete further reading/research? Specify.	☐	☐	
3. Has the student experienced any challenges in their research? Specify.	☐	☐	
3a. If yes, has the student overcome these challenges or have a plan in place?	☐	☐	
3b. If yes, have these challenges required any changes to their research question?	☐	☐	
4. Does the student require additional time before beginning the writing phase?	☐	☐	

Additional comments
....

Student signature:		Date:
Supervisor's signature:		Date:

Extended Essay progress form			**4**
Progress check			

Due by [   ] to the IBDP/EE Coordinator

Student name:		Supervisor:	

Subject:	

Refined research question:	

Progress check

Action	Yes	No	Supervisor's comments
1. Has the student presented some preliminary writing or shown portions of their essay for review and discussion?	☐	☐	
2. Does the student have a plan for completing the first draft (including the final structure and holiday plans)?	☐	☐	
3. Is the student on track to complete a full first draft by the scheduled date?	☐	☐	

Additional comments

Student signature:		Date:	
Supervisor's signature:		Date:	

Supervisory support emails

Below is a recommended process to follow in terms of supervisory sessions. The key aim is to enable both you and your supervisor to make the most of these sessions.

For Supervisors: Below is a list of support emails that an Extended Essay Coordinator could send out to supervisors at key junctures in the supervisory process. The timing of these support emails can be found in the exemplar calendar provided on page 79. These emails can complement and be blended into the three mandatory sessions that will form the basis for the completion of the Reflections on Planning and Progress Form (RPPF).

For Students: The emails below offer structural guidance for you in terms of things you should be working towards or prepared to discuss with your supervisor at key junctures in the Extended Essay process. It never hurts to go prepared to your supervisory sessions with the information or planning indicated below or at the very least request from your supervisor support along the lines indicated.

The first meeting

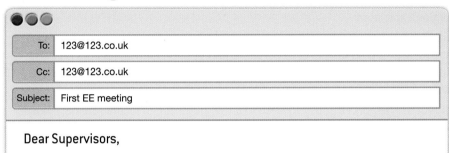

To:	123@123.co.uk
Cc:	123@123.co.uk
Subject:	First EE meeting

Dear Supervisors,

All students should be making appointments to come see you regarding Form 2 that needs to be handed in. The general expectation is that supervisors support them through a discussion of the initial stages of their Extended Essays. Below is a checklist of items you should consider discussing with them during this first meeting.

First session:	
Things to be prepared to discuss in your first supervisory session:	
Criteria	As a first step you should go over the subject-specific assessment criteria with your supervisor. Ensure you go through the subject-specific interpretation of criteria as there are slight differences in terms of how a criterion is interpreted from subject to subject. There may also be subject-specific expectations that you will need to meet (for example, in history the research question must not cover a period within the last ten years).
Research question	It is important for you to work with your supervisor in this initial meeting to narrow your topic/question down to a manageable scope (that is, capable of being covered in 4,000 words).
	It is also imperative that you investigate the viability of your topic with your supervisor. (For example, do you need special equipment? Are the resources available in the region/in school?)
	This is especially true if the nature of your question requires you to conduct primary research that is just **not** readily available (for example, theatre productions and fibre-optic equipment).
	It is also common for you to have chosen a wildly interesting but impractical question in the sense that there are little or no resources available in general. It is vital in such instances to heed the advice of your supervisor.
	It is important for you to remember at this juncture that if you wish to pursue a particular question then it is your responsibility ultimately. Under no circumstances should you expect your supervisor to prescribe or create a research question for you.

Exemplars	Ask your supervisor to issue you with an exemplar essay (or two) in your chosen subject. There are a number of A-grade exemplar essays on the IB's Online Curriculum Centre (OCC – occ.ibo.org) that your supervisor should have access to or which the school's IB Coordinator can grant access to if needs be. The same site contains examiner reports that shed useful light on good and bad approaches while also offering tips and recommendations. Your school is also likely to be in possession of other exemplar material (from previous cohorts, for example) so do ask.
Library	Ensure you speak with your school's librarian who is in a strong position to advise you in terms of existing in-school publications or online access to journals and the like that could prove useful.
Structure	Work with your supervisor to devise a plan as to how your research question could be structured or go to the session with a proposed structure you have in mind for review (chapter headings, for instance). Mind maps, flow charts and other models could prove useful here to help you visualize your essay's structure even at this early stage. It will also help with your research focus as you will know what areas need to be covered to successfully respond to your initial question/topic area.
Time-management	If you are finding it difficult to plan your time due to other assessment pressures or extra-curricular demands, then it may be useful to speak to your supervisor with regards creating a workable plan with you and helping you stick with it. A structured research timeline or more specific timetable will help you to see exactly what is required and when.
Resourcing	Start thinking about the resources you may need to either purchase or locate (online, in local libraries and so forth). It will also help to work with your supervisor on prioritizing your reading so you don't waste too much time on peripheral reading.

The second meeting

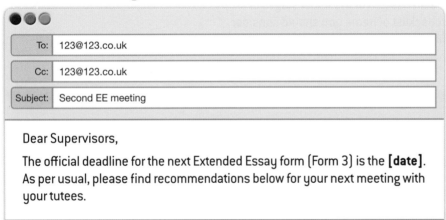

To:	123@123.co.uk
Cc:	123@123.co.uk
Subject:	Second EE meeting

Dear Supervisors,

The official deadline for the next Extended Essay form (Form 3) is the **[date]**. As per usual, please find recommendations below for your next meeting with your tutees.

Second session:	
Things to be prepared to discuss in your second supervisory session:	
Passivity	You may find that you have not done as much as you would have hoped since your first supervisory session. If this is the case, do discuss the reasons and causes for this with your supervisor and work with them to find ways to overcome or avoid this in future sessions. What is often helpful are stricter deadlines and another quick follow-up meeting in a week or two. The key here is to be honest and practical in your approach as the supervisor is there to guide you in these areas.

Reading	Be prepared to discuss your reading and/or research (for example, experiments and fieldwork) with your supervisor. Ideally, you should aim to comment on articles, chapters, journals, web pages and any other material you have researched.
	– What did you find out about the topic? Any surprises?
	– Any useful lines of thought or approaches to the question?
	Be wary of the common trap that most students find themselves in here, which is to assume that possessing materials or having done some preliminary scan for them is the same as having conducted research. The key here should be to be able to prove to your supervisor through your reading that the resources gathered are actually enough to substantiate your question. This is why the reading of resources or the conducting of experiments (where applicable) is important by this stage because it helps form the core of your research investigation. Being prepared and able to answer questions about your research is thus a useful exercise.
Notes	Ask yourself if you have a workable note-taking system in place. There is an assumption that you will be fine with simply reading the material gathered and will then write off the top of your head from memory. This is not a good approach to a pre-university research paper.
	Seeing as you are required to cite sources when you use them (or keep running footnotes) a note-taking system is essential. As a basic model, jotting down quotes or interesting points and the book title/page number(s) they came from is a minimum expectation when it comes to notes. Work with your supervisor on a note-taking system that works well for the purposes of your Extended Essay's chosen subject area.
Essay plan	It is very important for you to go over your essay plan with your supervisor or begin looking at options in terms of how to best structure it. This could be in the form of a mind-map, webbing and so forth. It will also help if you revisit your initial planning that was done in previous sessions with your supervisor and see what aspects may need further work or adapting to new discoveries you have made as a result of your ongoing reading/research.
	Once again, bear in mind that your supervisor's role is not to prescribe any one approach to your question but simply to ask probing questions to help you clarify an optimum essay plan.
Exemplars	Go over existing Extended Essays again so that you have a better idea with regards the scope of the paper you are going to finally create along with different approaches to its overall structure (that is, what parts it may end up containing).
	It may also be a useful exercise to mark a pre-existing essay and then review the rationale for your marking with your supervisor. This allows you to engage with the assessment criteria first hand and thus write your own essay with them firmly in mind.
Time-management	A usual problem with Extended Essays is time-management. Many students believe (erroneously) that they will have plenty of time to complete it later. Work with your supervisor on this and be prepared to make some adjustments to your normal routines to accommodate any delays or issues with your EE thus far. Bear in mind these adjustments are necessary but temporary. Often setting aside one free period every two weeks to work on your EE helps significantly. Work with your supervisor to formally set something on your timetable. Sticking to deadlines will ensure you can get this task done so that you can focus on other work required as part of your studies.
Writing	It is not essential for you to have written anything yet in terms of the actual EE, but it also does not hurt to have started jotting things down that you can then build the rest of your EE around. Bear in mind that writing proper should begin in the next few months and in earnest during the end-of-year break. The more versions you are able to write, the better off your EE will be. You can't work with nothing so do commit to getting started on writing after this supervisory session.
Research question	Tweaking of questions is perfectly fine though you should avoid wholesale changes to your topic area/question at this juncture as you will struggle to complete the work in time otherwise.

Extended Essay café (coming soon) [optional]:

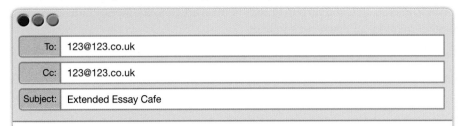

To:	123@123.co.uk
Cc:	123@123.co.uk
Subject:	Extended Essay Cafe

We will be running an EE café on the [date]. You will be asked to present your research and findings to date in a formal presentation setting to your peers, supervisors and parents. As a result, you should have been actively working on your EE so that you have something meaningful to present.

The purpose of the EE café is to get you focused on your investigation and provide you with an opportunity to communicate your research, discoveries, challenges and so forth to the rest of the cohort. This will be in the style of a Masters/PhD presentation to a university board so you will have this practice experience also. It will also double up as a meeting for you to complete Form 4.

The third meeting
Extended Essay—draft submission stage

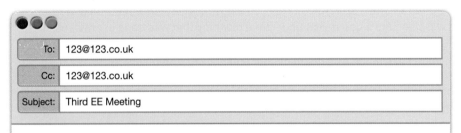

To:	123@123.co.uk
Cc:	123@123.co.uk
Subject:	Third EE Meeting

Students will be expected to submit a complete working draft of their Extended Essay to you by the **[date]**. This "draft" should contain all sections of the EE as specified in the marking criteria.

Third session:	
Things you should expect to discuss with your supervisor in the third session:	
Marking	You should be expecting to receive feedback on your first full draft of your EE from your supervisor. Be prepared to discuss ways you can improve across all the assessment criteria. These can be found on the Online Curriculum Centre (OCC) which contains an online version. Ask your supervisors about this so your feedback can be specific and focused on the actual criteria.
Process	Your supervisor is expected to comment on each of the marking criteria. It may be the case that they have annotated the essay itself with general remarks in line with the assessment criteria so that you have an idea of the specific areas they are concerned with. Although supervisors can make suggestions for improvement you must **not** expect them to edit your work.
Criteria	*Specific support for the assessment criteria can be found in Chapter 7: Assessment (maximizing marks). You may wish to review this chapter in addition to any materials provided by your supervisor.*

Timeline	Ideally, you should expect to have your EE back within two weeks of submission, although this will depend on your individual school's calendar. You should aim to give yourself at least four weeks between the feedback on first draft and final submission so that you have enough time to make meaningful improvements and changes. A focused timeframe will ensure that you stay focused on this task and do not exceed the maximum recommended time for this work.

Supervisor guidance: The final meeting
Preparing for the viva voce

To:	123@123.co.uk
Cc:	123@123.co.uk
Subject:	The Viva Voce

Dear Supervisors,

This is the final formal requirement for Extended Essays so please read the information provided carefully.

You should spend from **15 to 20 minutes** conducting this concluding interview (viva voce).

A series of questions have already been provided for you (Session 3 on page 93) but feel free to ask any other related questions you feel appropriate. The idea is to get the students talking about their EEs, the process, the methods followed, the struggles, frustrations and challenges encountered, any interesting discoveries and so on. It is also our primary means of **ensuring that the students have not plagiarized** (as they should be able to speak about their EEs with confidence and not umm and ah when asked about specific sections or sources).

What the viva voce is not:

The viva voce form is not an opportunity to voice frustrations regarding a student's lack of engagement and poor work ethic. The focus should be on the process of writing the Extended Essay. Your comments therefore should match accordingly. Also, do not include any comments about medical issues and special circumstances that may have affected performance as that is handled separately by the IB Diploma Coordinator.

Comments:

Your first line should mention the fact that in your professional assessment the work is the student's own. The rest of the information you provide will help the examiners with Criterion E: Engagement (6 marks) so focus comments on that area. Do mention any interesting approaches to the essay that the student was not able to embed in the essay proper (novel ways of carrying out the investigation, work ethic, research not present in the bibliography, student engagement with the topic and so forth).

The three mandatory sessions

Basics	
1. How long are these sessions?	As a whole, a supervisor should spend no more than five hours (give or take) with you over the duration of the Extended Essay process.
	These hours can be divided into quick 10–15 minute catch-up sessions followed by longer 30–40 minute sessions for the three mandatory interview sessions that will inform your Reflections on Planning and Progress Form (RPPF).
2. Are the sessions recorded?	There is now an expectation that at least three sessions take place after which you will write reflections on the RPPF. These are usually broken down into:
	a. an introductory meeting
	b. a meeting halfway through the process (usually after the student has completed their research and has begun some preliminary writing or is about to)
	c. a meeting that is part of the concluding interview (viva voce).
	The supervisor must sign and date this form shortly after each session.
3. Are these sessions assessed?	The sessions themselves are not assessed but they will help to highlight the student's ability to reflect on the research process.
	The new criteria **award six marks** for student engagement with the research process (Criterion E: Engagement).
	The supervisory sessions should therefore aim to help you maximize on the award of these grades by supporting you with things such as planning and structure, appropriate methodologies and approaches while also encouraging you to reflect on research challenges encountered and possible solutions found.

Guidance for mandatory sessions

The following table is intended as a guide for you and your supervisor with regards to the three mandatory sessions. For students it will be useful to be aware of the types of things you should be preparing for in anticipation of the mandatory and documented meetings with your supervisor.

Session 1	Examples of guiding questions
● Initial ideas ● Topics ● Possible approaches ● Research question(s) ● Ethical considerations	**1.** Why have you chosen this topic/event/figure/case study as the focus of your RQ? **2.** How is your question appropriate to the chosen subject? **3.** Why is this RQ worthy of investigation? **4.** Have you considered whether to pursue a primary or secondary research approach to respond to your RQ? Why is that the best approach? **5.** What contradictions, concerns or controversies are you already aware of in relation to your RQ? **6.** If in history, does your RQ cover a period at least ten years from today? **7.** Is there enough material readily available to support such an essay? **8.** What sources do you think may be useful and why (letters, newspapers, interviews, histories and so on)? **9.** What may be some problems in arriving at a conclusion to your EE (for example, reliability of sources and bias of accounts)? **10.** Are there any ethical considerations you need to take into account? Will these affect your research and how do you propose to overcome them?

Session 2	Examples of guiding questions
• Follow-up • Research findings • Reading completed (and pending) • Organization and structure Next-step planning	**1.** Have you made any adjustments to your initial RQ since Session 1? Why? **2.** Which sources have you utilized thus far in terms of your research? **3.** What perspectives have you been made aware of through your reading? **4.** Is there a discernible pattern or approach that dominates? **5.** What aspects of your reading have surprised, impressed, shocked or challenged you? **6.** What material have you rejected from your list of sources? Why? **7.** What areas do you feel need further exploration? **8.** Are there aspects of the material you are struggling with? **9.** Have you had any issues with your time management? How have you addressed this? **10.** What ideas do you have with regards to the layout of your Extended Essay (chapters, headings and so forth)? **11.** What next steps do you consider vital for the completion of your Extended Essay?
Session 3	**Examples of guiding questions**
• Viva voce • Conclusions • Writing process • Challenges or setbacks • Academic honesty	**1.** What conclusions did you arrive at during the research and writing of your EE? Were there any surprises? **2.** What would you consider to be the most (and least) rewarding aspect of your research and writing process? **3.** What figures or illustrations did you include? Why did you choose those? **4.** Which source contradicted the general ideas of your research? In what way specifically did the source contradict them? Did you include it? Why? Why not? **5.** Which of your sources did you find to be the most helpful? Why? **6.** Select a few sections from the work and ask the student questions pertaining to their meaning, why they were used and their relevance (for example, why did you select this source to support your points or what do you think X was getting at when he said "Y"?) **7.** What have you learned about your topic from researching and writing about it? **8.** What challenges did you encounter when researching and writing the EE? How did you go about overcoming them? **9.** What unanswered question are you left with? **10.** How successful do you believe you've been with regards to answering your RQ? **11.** Is there anything that contributed to the EE that is not immediately evident in the essay itself (such as museum visits and email exchanges with participants, scientists and authors).

The Extended Essay Café

Supervisor guidance: What is it?

An Extended Essay Café is an opportunity for students to formally present their Extended Essay research findings to date to a panel of supervisors and/or coordinators.

The timing of the EE Café can be found in the exemplar calendar on page 80.

Rationale:

Running an EE Café is an excellent way for a school's coordinators and supervisors to ensure that all students submitting an Extended Essay have made suitable progress with regards to the research (and any initial writing) phase of their essays. An EE Café usually takes place before the end of the first year of the IB Diploma and as such is perfectly situated to act as a check on progress while also an opportunity to help students create a road-map in terms of what needs to be done during the holiday period. It is also an opportunity for schools to identify those students who have not been on task and are behind schedule so as to implement necessary remedial strategies and support.

By making it a formal occasion, as opposed to one-on-one supervisory sessions, the Café helps galvanize student interest and compels them to focus their efforts before the end-of-year break. By inviting parents along also, it helps enfranchise a major stakeholder in the students' lives, demystifies the entire process for parents and gains access to another key group of people who can more often than not offer additional insights, support, resources and advice to the students engaged with the Extended Essay process.

Format:

You will be given five minutes to present your most up-to-date findings and research related to your Extended Essays before a panel of specialist judges (such as coordinators and experienced supervisors), your peers and parents. Schools with large cohorts may wish to have multiple sessions running, each with its own panel and allocation of students.

You will be required to inform the panel of the following:

1. Subject and research question

2. Background (what your EE is about, key issues addressed and so forth)

3. Research conducted thus far and planned research for the summer (such as a summary of one to two chapters/sections)

4. Possible chapter headings (or a working outline of the final contents page)

5. Problems encountered and solutions found (where applicable)

6. Bibliography (accurately referenced sources using an agreed upon style)

Requirements:

✓ All students must have a visual presentation (such as PowerPoint or Prezi) where the above points are visually represented. The panel will be looking to see that all students have workable research questions, a draft essay plan and a properly formulated bibliography.

✓ Students are free to present a summation of the content of their
EEs in whichever manner they choose.

✓ Students must bring along Form 4 (page 86) filled in with all relevant
details for submission to supervisors/panel.

Supervisors:

Supervisors are invited to attend the session(s) where they can also ask
questions and listen into their tutees' presentations. This session can also count
as a formal interview and an opportunity to fill in **Form 4** (see page 85).

Extended Essay Café checklist

Component	Comments
Research question: Does the question sound workable? Is it narrow enough to be completed in 4,000 words? Does it have a clear focus? Can it be resourced?	
Structure: Usually good to see some chapter headings that indicate organization of the essay into sections. Check to see if chapters are relevant and of a reasonable number, as then each will be too brief to be meaningful.	
Content: The one chapter or aspect they elaborate on should convince you they know something about their topic or are able to develop a line of argument. Though background information can be included it should not be the focus of the entire presentation.	
Bibliography: Alphabetical, spelling correct, capitals for titles, publication date and location, author and so forth are all correct. If you know about the topic then add anything about relevance or quality of sources.	
Plans: Do they have a workable plan for the summer? Add anything to this if you feel the student's work to date is vague or nebulous.	

Exemplar EE Café presentation

Below is an exemplar presentation completed for a history Extended Essay.

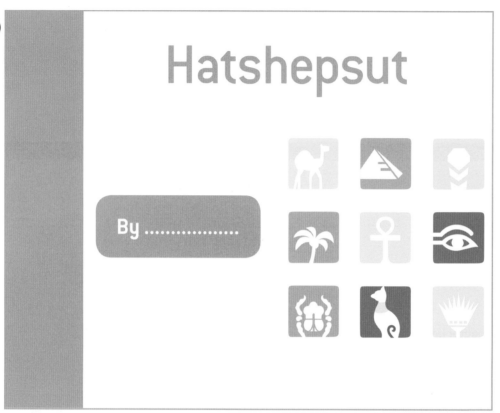

Introductory slide listing your name and a summative heading related to your research question.

To what extent does Hatshepsut owe her accession to the throne of Egypt to the appropriation of religious imagery?

Explicitly state your research question so the panel knows what your essay is going to be about. This should be in the form of a question.

3

Background

Who was Hatshepsut?

- She was the first female Pharaoh.
- After the death of her father she married her step-brother Thutmose II and had a daughter with him.
- When he died the throne passed to his son and Hatshepsut's nephew Thutmose III.
- He was an infant so she ruled as queen regent. During this time she took the throne.

Provide some background or context to help your audience understand your question better. This could take the form of quick facts but should ideally link back to the main research question.

4

Background

What did she do?

- She became Pharaoh and gave herself a male appearance (for example, attaching a ceremonial beard to her chin).
- Her reign was one of peace and prosperity with an effective government, expanding foreign trade and artist rebirth.

❺

Table of contents

Introduction
- Background

Chapter 1 – Political factors
  - Political roles
  - Social context of women

Chapter 2 – Religion
  - Cult of Amun
  - Divine Birth

Chapter 3 – Economic factors
  - Voyage to Punt

Chapter 4 – Domestic policies
  - Building programmes

Chapter 5 – Iconography
  - Change from queen to king

> Here you should present your proposed table of contents. It could also take the form of a mind map. The key point here is to indicate to the viewers what areas (or sub-topics) you are planning on covering to successfully answer your research question.

❻

Chapter 1

Chapter 1
  - Political factors
  - Political roles
  - Social context of women
  - Role as queen regent

- Before the death of her husband she had an array of titles. To a degree, she was able to manipulate these by giving herself such titles as "God's Wife".
- At the time it was socially acceptable for women to rule as "King's mother" or "Queen regent" in the stead of a infant son. Although Thutmose III was not her son Hatshepsut took on the role of Queen Regent.

> Select two of the chapter headings (or stands from your mind map) to elaborate upon in more detail. Here you should be trying to convince your audience that you've done the requisite research and know your stuff.

7

Chapter 2

Chapter 2
- – Religion
- – Cult of Amun
- – Divine Birth
- Amun is the god of life and Ra is the god of the sun. In a tactical move Hatshepsut joined these two to create a chief diety.
- The Divine Birth is based on the story of Isis and Osiris. Hatshepsut could not rule as a female by herself without religious security.

8

Bibliography

BOOKS
- Monderson, F. (2011). *Hatshepsut's temple at Deir El Bahari*. New York: SuMon Publishers.
- Robins, G. (1993). *Women In Ancient Egypt*. Cambridge: Harvard University Press.
- Roerig, R. D. (2005). *Hatchepsut – From queen to Pharaoh*. New York: The Metropolitan Museum of Art.
- Tyldesley, J. (1998). *Hatchepsut The Female Pharaoh*. England: Penguin Group.

ARTICLES AND WEBSITES
- Ann, C. (2011, July 14). *Hatshepsut*. Retrieved April 2, 2012, from Teen Ink: http://www.teenink.com/nonfiction/academic/article/348279/Hatshepsut/
- Brown, C. (2009). The King Herself. *National Geographic*, http://ngm.nationalgeographic.com/2009/04/hatshepsut/brown-text.html.
- Lewis, J. J. (n.d.). *Hatshepsut and Ancient Egypt's Theology of Kingship*. Retrieved April 3, 2012, from About.com: http://womenshistory.about.com/od/hatshepsut/a/king_theology.htm
- Nosotro, R. (2010, October 9). *"His Majesty, Herself – Queen Hatshepsut"*. Retrieved April 3, 2012, from HyperHistory.net: http://www.hyperhistory.net/apwh/bios/b1hatshepsut_3hm.htm
- Tyldesley, D. J. (2011, February 12). *Hatshepsut and Tuthmosis: A Royal Feud?* Retrieved April 2, 2012, from BBC: www.bbc.co.uk/history/ancient/egyptians/hatshepsut_01.shtml
- Walker, R. J. (1997). World Civilizations: A Comparative Study. 67.
- Wilson, E. B. (2006, September). *The Queen Who Would Be King*. Retrieved April 2, 2012, from Smithsonian magazine: www.smithsonianmag.com/historyarchaeology/The-Queen-Who-Would-Be-King.html

Show your bibliography (to date) using an approved referencing style (for example, APA or MLA). The key here is to show to your audience that you know how to correctly reference source material.

9

Plans

1. Continue to consolidate my plan for each chapter with sufficient evidence.
2. Reading Robins' Book: *Women in Ancient Egypt*
3. Complete a source analysis of Tyldesley.
4. Write first draft.

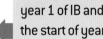
Provide an outline for your plans during the holidays between year 1 of IB and the start of year 2.

10

Problems

- One main problem I had was with the sources. Due to the nature of the topic it is heavily based on secondary sources and contemporaneous interpretation. To overcome this I had to read a range of articles and books to create a suitably balanced reading.
- Had to acknowledge the lack of primary source materials outside Hatshepsut's building works. Possible limitation for history EE.
- Mr Kosta is very demanding. ☺

Highlight any problems you may have encountered at all stages of the EE process, be they the defining of the research question, the locating of appropriate resources, problems with any experiments and the like. Often, the panel/audience will be able to offer support and guidance to help you.

7: Assessment (maximizing marks)

The Extended Essay assessment criteria

The criteria against which all Extended Essays will be assessed from September 2016 (first assessment 2018) are as follows:

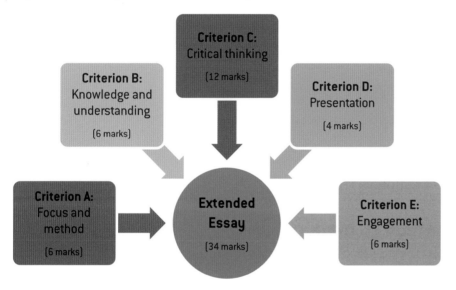

This chapter is focused on how to navigate the assessment criteria so as to maximize the marks awarded. As a general rule it is useful to bear in mind that if the essay does not meet the criteria, then it cannot access the full marks. The criteria act as the goal posts so it is crucial that you (and your supervisor) understand what they ask of you and also how to go about ensuring you meet them.

> **Golden rule:** Know the criteria

The strands

The IB has set out a series of *strands* that act as the core focus of each criterion. In order to attain the highest grades a student needs to meet these for each of the criteria. These strands are as follows:

Criterion	Strands
A. Focus and method	• Topic • Research question • Methodology
B. Knowledge and understanding	• Context • Communication
C. Critical thinking	• Research • Analysis • Discussion and evaluation
D. Presentation	• Structure • Layout
E. Engagement	• Research focus • Planning and process

Each criterion will be elaborated upon in the following section with suggested approaches, useful tips and explanations relating to the strands offered across a wide range of IB subjects.

Criterion A: Focus and method (6 marks)

This criterion has a number of aspects that are closely aligned with it:

- Choice of topic
- Research question
- Methodology and/or sources utilized

The introduction

The introduction to the essay is your best friend when it comes to Criterion A as it is the perfect place to outline how almost all of the strands for Criterion A are to be covered in the body of the essay that follows. Due to this, it is advisable to write the introduction as *a separate and clearly labelled section* so that examiners can identify how you've gone about meeting the strands for Criterion A.

Although you can certainly create an outline of what your essay may include and look like contents-wise at the outset of the EE process, it is recommended that you finalize the writing of the introduction last once the essay has taken shape.

Question and Answer

Question: What do I include in my introduction?

Answer: There are four core things to explicitly mention in your introduction: the research question, some context with regards your topic, why it is worthy of investigation and the methodological approach and/or source material you've used to arrive at your conclusion.

INTRODUCTION	
INCLUDE	**DETAILS**
Research question (RQ)	Aside from on the title page, it is advisable to explicitly refer to your research question in the introduction. Do not simply list it but rather blend it into the prose of your introduction (for example, "This paper seeks to explore the extent to which …").
	Also, bear in mind that the conclusion to your RQ **must not** be obvious but should rather involve a degree of research and analysis on your part. Questions that are largely of the yes/no variant, or that lead to a simple conclusion, are not appropriate.
	Usually questions that begin with "who" or "what" lead to poor investigations as seen in the examples below:
	History EE on the Munich Agreement (1938) • RQ: What did Chamberlain hope to achieve from the Munich Agreement in 1938? • Conclusion: He sought to avoid war with Nazi Germany.
	Visual Arts EE on H.R. Giger's Work • RQ: Which techniques did HR Giger find more emblematic for his work? • Conclusion: Airbrush
	Economics EE on the public listing of a company • RQ: Who stands to benefit the most from the public listing of Company X? • Conclusion: The shareholders
	(See Chapter 2, pages 10–17 for more on how to devise good research questions.)
Context	You should always situate your RQ within any existing theories, approaches or evaluations that underpin your topic as a whole.
	For example:
	➤ Are there pre-existing interpretations of the "text" you're writing about?
	➤ What pre-existing theories are there as to the cause of an event you're investigating?
	➤ What conclusions do the major analytical tools or techniques related to your topic point to?
	➤ What alternative schools of thought have been applied to the analysis of the topic you have in mind (for example, psychoanalytical and deconstructivism)?
	➤ Are there alternative methodological approaches to your question?

Worthiness	It is imperative that you mention why your question is worthy of investigation or why we the readers should care about the potential conclusion(s).
	Types of things that would be suitable here include:
	✓ Offers a different interpretation to existing ones
	✓ Is a contemporaneous and/or controversial topic that demands investigation (you must state the nature of the controversy)
	✓ Has relevance or application in real-world dynamics
	✓ Has often been erroneously represented (for example, through film adaptations or media sound bites)
	✓ Is an often poorly explored field, area or topic of investigation
	✓ Is of critical importance to the reading of a "text"
	✓ Challenges existing assumptions or interpretations relating to the topic (or texts)
	✓ Is assessing the validity of existing assumptions or interpretations
	✓ Utilizes a different methodological approach in the hope of gleaning new insight into a given topic
	✓ Evaluates different methodological approaches in the hope of deducing a "best" one (that is, for example, being more accurate or more reliable)
	✓ Testing existing theories within a specific sample set
	Types of things that are **not** suitable here include:
	✗ Liking the subject/topic
	✗ It is interesting (stating this is not sufficient as you must frame what makes it so, ideally in relation to one of the tick points above)
	✗ Your parents are fond of the subject matter/topic
	✗ Your teacher/supervisor instructed you to research it (this is not allowed under the IB rules governing the EE to begin with)
	✗ Your elder sibling or friend is studying this at university
Methodological approach (or source-based approach)	Your introduction should offer an outline into your chosen methodological (or source-based) approach so that the examiner is clear on *how* you went about answering the RQ.
	[Methodology] Consider the following also:
	a. Why was this method chosen?
	b. What is it about this method that helps answer the question (for example, greater reliability, repeatability, sample size, margin of error or industry standard)?
	[Source-based] Consider the following:
	a. Why were the sources chosen (for example, they establish the traditional interpretative approaches that you will evaluate or challenge, offer diverse evaluative approaches or provide a new interpretative framework)?
	b. How are you going to use or respond to their claims (for example, challenge, affirm, prove or test)?

AVOID	DETAILS
Descriptive backgrounds	Avoid narrating the extensive background of your chosen topic as this often is either irrelevant or ends up being purely descriptive filler. **Keep it to the point and relevant to the focus of your RQ.** Example of poor introductions: **History EE on Hitler's rise to power** • Candidate mentions details relating to Hitler's childhood and upbringing. **English EE on representations of justice in Harper Lee's *To Kill a Mockingbird*** • Candidate offers biographical information on Harper Lee. **Biology EE on optical isomers** • Candidate offers an account of the historical development of research on said topic beginning with Louis Pasteur's early pioneering work.
Biography	Biographical data, although useful under certain circumstances, is usually a poor substitute for proper research and analysis into a given topic. If anything, it often leads to a reductionist approach whereby the work of a given individual is summarized as an extension of their actual life. It has next to no place in the EE as a whole, and, therefore, should be avoided in the introduction as well.
Political or religious stance	The introduction (or EE as a whole) is no place to outline your personal political or religious agenda.
Personal pronouns	As the EE is intended to be an academic-style research paper the use of the personal pronouns ("I", "my" and so on) is best avoided on the whole.

For an exemplar introduction, refer to Chapter 5: Writing Essays
Essay (page 64).

Criterion B: Knowledge and understanding (6 marks)

This criterion effectively evaluates how well you demonstrate content knowledge and understanding of the key issues, debates, theories, and arguments that surround your chosen topic. It also measures how fluently and accurately you use the command terms (or terminology) and concepts of your chosen subject. This also includes demonstrating knowledge of any subject-specific modes of analysis, preferred methodological approaches or styles and any evaluative or interpretative frameworks. Lastly, high marks in this criterion are awarded if the choice of resources is consistently relevant and befitting of an academic research paper in the chosen subject.

The table below highlights some other subject-specific requirements for
a range of subjects:

Subjects	Requirements	Avoid
Literature (Group 1)	✓ Knowledge and understanding of primary text(s) used is the key here. This is demonstrated through how well key passages, quotes or lines from the original text(s) are used to back up the claims made. ✓ Some context should be offered. This could take the form of an acknowledgment of alternate textual readings or interpretations from established scholars. It is always advisable to argue how your approach agrees, differs or challenges these pre-established viewpoints.	✗ Excessive historical and/or biographical background information ✗ Do not include definitions in footnotes ✗ Do not include images that are not referenced in the body of the essay
Language (Group 1)	✓ Some context should be offered that showcases any existing theories or approaches to your chosen text(s) or language aspects. ✓ Demonstrate in what way your topic is of relevance or of particular interest/significance to the target language.	✗ Personal experiences or opinions (unless you fall into the target audience of the language) ✗ Do not include definitions in footnotes ✗ Do not include images that are not referenced in the body of the essay
Language and culture (Group 2)	✓ Some consideration of the context into which the topic is situated (for example, cultural context) ✓ An understanding of the implications of your topic to the wider culture or language chosen ✓ Some of your research material should include (or be based on) primary sources	✗ Excessive historical and/or biographical background information ✗ Do not include definitions in footnotes ✗ Do not include images that are not referenced in the body of the essay
Literature (Group 2)	See Literature Group 1.	See Literature Group 1.
Business management (Group 3)	✓ Source material chosen should all be relevant to your topic/RQ. ✓ Situate your topic/RQ within the wider business context. ✓ Accurate and consistent use of business terminology and concepts should be present throughout the essay. ✓ Offer explanations and definitions for complex terms or concepts used (specifically in relation to how you use them in your essay).	✗ Do not include definitions in footnotes. ✗ Do not include images that are not referenced in the body of the essay.

Economics (Group 3)	✓ Use of relevant economic theory and models is the key here.	✗ Do not include a separate section on background theory or terminology.
	✓ Any references to background theory should be integrated within the body of the essay itself. Ideally this should appear at the exact point where it is referred to as opposed to in a different section.	✗ Do not include definitions in footnotes.
		✗ Do not use generic diagrams or graphs.
		✗ Do not include images that are not referenced in the body of the essay
	✓ Clearly indicating how the economic theory and data gathered is used to answer the RQ is also essential.	
	✓ Real-world data should underpin all arguments and be the basis of any application of economic models.	
	✓ Diagrams should be correctly labelled and supported with evidence through in-text analysis and commentary so as to demonstrate their relevance.	
Geography (Group 3)	✓ Explain the terms and concepts used within the body of your essay.	✗ Do not explain terms and concepts in footnotes or as separate sections.
	✓ Use acknowledged geographical sources as much as possible.	✗ Do not include definitions in footnotes.
	✓ Include only relevant source material.	✗ Do not include images that are not referenced in the body of the essay.
	✓ Support your points/arguments with relevant source material at all times.	
	✓ Diagrams, graphs, maps and so forth should all be correctly labelled and supported by solid geographical evidence (either primary or secondary in nature).	
Global politics (Group 3)	✓ Establish clear links between your chosen topic and the political theories, figures or institutions that underpin it.	✗ Do not include definitions in footnotes.
	✓ Place your topic within the wider political context by showing how they relate.	✗ Do not include images that are not referenced in the body of the essay.
	✓ Demonstrate an awareness of how socio-cultural biases can affect the political issue being investigated.	
	✓ It is vital that you demonstrate a solid grasp of the subject's terminology as taught in the IBDP course.	
	✓ Ensure you provide ongoing analyses of the data and source material you've utilized.	

History (Group 3)	✓ All source material used in the body of the essay must help develop an argument and be relevant to the research question. ✓ Place your research question within the wider historical context (e.g. link it to causation, implications, impact, etc). ✓ Accurately employ historical command terms and concepts. ✓ Ensure all your information is factual and accurate.	✗ Do not simply use source material to recount events or tell a narrative. ✗ Do not base your EE on events within the last ten years (or the maximum you can get for Criterion B is 4 marks). ✗ Do not include definitions in footnotes. ✗ Do not include images that are not referenced in the body of the essay.
Information technology in a global society (ITGS) (Group 3)	✓ Offer a clear explanation of the IT system your essay is exploring along with accurately cited and labelled diagrams and images. ✓ All visual material should be labelled, cited accurately and referred to in the body of the essay. ✓ Use correct IT terminology fluently in the body of the essay.	✗ Do not include images that are not referenced in the body of the essay. ✗ Do not include definitions in footnotes.
Psychology (Group 3)	✓ Offer an evaluation and/or commentary of the studies chosen based on any cultural, ethical, gender and methodological factors that may have contributed or influenced them. ✓ Accurately and consistently utilize the terms and concepts associated with the IBDP psychology course. ✓ Base your essay on relevant source material (ideally of an academic nature).	✗ Generally avoid using sources that do not fit the academic model for psychological studies. ✗ Do not include definitions in footnotes. ✗ Do not include images that are not referenced in the body of the essay.
Natural sciences (Group 4)	✓ Seeing as secondary source materials are a bare minimum requirement, all essays should ensure that all materials are from reputable scientific sources and clearly relevant to the investigation. ✓ Correctly utilize any scientific terms and apply them correctly in the body of the essay. ✓ Make appropriate and consistent use of science-specific units of measurement, symbols and so forth. ✓ Explain any technical terms in relation to how you use them in your essay.	✗ Do not make excessive use of science jargon (clarity is preferred above all). ✗ Do not provide step-by-step, recipe-style lists of resources used in experimental work and overly detailed procedurals (remember the Extended Essay is not an IA). ✗ Do not include definitions in footnotes. ✗ Do not include images that are not referenced in the body of the essay.

Mathematics (Group 5)	✓ Only mathematics that is relevant to the specific research question should be used in the body of the essay.	✗ Do not include wider mathematical knowledge if not directly relevant to the chosen research question.
	✓ It is generally advised to pitch an EE in mathematics to an audience of people who have anything ranging from a strong interest to advanced knowledge of mathematics. This often means writing in such a way that the argument, as demonstrated by the mathematics used, is clear. This involves doing the mathematics and showing all the steps behind the reasoning.	✗ Do not draw conclusions from mathematics without having first shown the working out in the body of the essay.
		✗ Do not include definitions in footnotes.
		✗ Do not include images that are not referenced in the body of the essay.
	✓ If complex theorems are used, always accompany them with an example to illustrate what you mean.	
The arts (Group 6)	✓ Always situate your research question within a wider social, historical or cultural context (this is not the same as providing lengthy background information).	✗ Avoid relying on subjective, opinion-based accounts.
	✓ Demonstrate an awareness of any existing theories, approaches, dialogue or criticism relevant to the specific arts subject and topic.	✗ Avoid including lengthy biographical or historical background information.
		✗ Do not include definitions in footnotes.
	✓ Evaluate your source material for reliability and validity, commenting on any limitations.	✗ Do not include images that are not referenced in the body of the essay.
	✓ Ensure you are consistent in your usage of subject-specific terminology and any specific language (for example, musical notation, stage terminology and visual arts techniques).	

Knowledge and understanding checklist

The worksheet below includes essential questions that all students should aim to respond to in order to maximize the grades awarded for Criterion B: Knowledge and understanding.

1. Have you supported key claims in your work with appropriate (ideally academic) source material?	YES ☐	NO ☐

CHECK: List your sources and then evaluate each one for reliability and validity. It should pass the following questioning if it's to be deemed of academic value:

a. Does your data come from approved or acknowledged sources? (Remember: blogs, general websites, Wikipedia and the like do not usually qualify.)

b. If your data comes from primary research, have you followed an approved or acknowledged methodology in terms of data collection? (Check with your supervisor if the method adheres to the subject's research guidelines.)

Tip

If the majority of your source material does not pass the above checks, consider finding alternate sources that do. Some of your sources can be non-academic in nature though care should be taken when using them in your work. As a minimum, acknowledge their limitations in your writing.

2. Have you assessed the value and limitations of your source material in your writing? (See Chapter 3.4.1 on pages 45–8 for help with this.)	YES	☐		NO	☐
3. Have you situated your research question within a wider context? *For example (psychology):* If your question explores the relationship between video games and violent behaviour in young males, have you shown an awareness of wider theories governing violence in males?	YES	☐		NO	☐
4. Have you accurately labelled all images, graphs, diagrams, maps and so on that you may have used?	YES	☐		NO	☐
5. Have you used subject-specific terminology (or conceptual language) accurately throughout your essay?	YES	☐		NO	☐

Tip

If you've used a technical term in a particular way, it helps to define your particular usage of it in the body of your work.

Also, complex terms benefit from a brief definition for the sake of clarity or an illustrative example to help the reader follow your train of thought.

6. Is your content accurate and factual at all times? (For example, measurements, dates, events, characters and so on are all correct.)	YES	☐		NO	☐
7. Does your method of analysis adhere to the subject's acknowledged conventions? (Check with your supervisor to ensure that your approach meets the subject's general guidelines.)	YES	☐		NO	☐
8. Where appropriate, does your essay meet the IB's ethical guidelines?	YES	☐		NO	☐

Criterion C: Critical thinking (12 marks)

This criterion has the most marks allocated to it for the very simple reason that the critical evaluation of the evidence in order to produce a reasoned argument and sound conclusion is the key focus of any research paper.

There are three key strands that need to be met in order to score high marks under this criterion:

a. Relevance of research

- All research materials gathered and used are clearly relevant to the research question posed.

b. Analysis of research findings

- The research findings are effectively analysed so as to produce a reasoned argument. Any developing analyses are well-supported by relevant evidence.

c. Discussion and evaluation of evidence

- A coherent and well-reasoned argument is developed that is supported by the evidence presented. What's more, a critical evaluation of the source material is present.

Knowledge and understanding	• Is your content knowledge accurate and is the source material used to support your claims relevant to the RQ at all times (see Criterion B for more)?
	• This is a basic expectation since any inaccuracies in content knowledge or irrelevant source material will diminish the potential for good analysis to emerge.
	• This includes responding to the "who", "what", "where", "how" and "why" questions as well as being able to describe events, processes and methods used accurately.

Application and analysis	• What does your research (primary and/or secondary) indicate with regards to your RQ?
	• Why did you choose that particular method or approach to answer the RQ? You should consider the suitability of your approach in the main body.
	• Are you able to point out any inherent contradictions or alternative viewpoints that need to be considered?
	• What limitations or weaknesses have you identified in your source material or methodological approach to the RQ?
	• Have you developed mini-analyses or arrived at micro-conclusions to each point you raised in the essay?

Synthesis and evaluation	• As a result of your research, what have you determined is the core answer (or multiple answers as the case may be) to your RQ?
	• Are there any aspects or factors you have not taken into account that need mentioning in your conclusion?
	• How definitive a conclusion can you arrive at? What would help make it more definitive?
	• How far does your conclusion differ from or challenge conventional wisdom or approaches?
	• Are your conclusions consistent with your argument as it develops in the main body?

Avoid	• Evaluations that are based on narrative or descriptive accounts.
	• Embedding new information in your final, concluding evaluation.
	• Basing your final evaluation on personal opinion or unsupported claims.
	• Drawing a conclusion at odds with your argument as it develops in the main body.
	• Failing to omit any mention of limitations in terms of your approach. It is good academic practice to recognize any shortcomings in your method or approach.

Critical thinking skills

In order to demonstrate that critical thinking has taken place in your essay, you should aim to have answered the following questions in the body of your work.

Criterion D: Presentation (4 marks)

It is important to bear in mind that the Extended Essay is a formal piece of academic writing and as such must be presented using the agreed-upon conventions of independently written research papers.

The IB prescribes a set of aspects that must be included as part of the Extended Essay. These are as follows:

- Title Page
- Table of contents
- Page numbers
- Font use
- Spacing
- Referencing (citations and bibliography)
- Word count

The following sections will guide you through each presentation requirement. A checklist is also provided for your use on page 132.

Title page (or cover page)

Consider your title page like the front of a book. It should bear some key information pertaining to your Extended Essay in line with the IB's expectations.

Title pages should include the following:

a. Title (optional)	A brief heading giving a summative description of what the essay is about is an optional extra you may wish to include. The best way to do this is to convert your RQ into a title that captures the key focus of the essay.
	For example:
	RQ: In what ways does Jane Austen express her attitudes to the themes of love and marriage inherent in her work *Pride and Prejudice*?
	Title: Austen's Attitudes to Marriage in Pride and Prejudice
	NOTE: The RQ often acts as the title also so this step is purely optional.
b. Research question (RQ)	When writing your RQ there are a few things to consider:
	1. Ensure it is the RQ that appears in other sections of your essay (for example, the introduction).
	2. Ensure it is the question being answered in the conclusion (as opposed to a variant of it).
	3. Ensure the spelling is correct and grammar accurate (and it ends with a question mark).
c. Subject	Ensure you've specified which subject the essay belongs to.
	GROUP 1
	For Group 1 (language and literature A) based essays you will also need to specify which category it belongs in:
	Category 1: Studies of Literary Works (all works originally written in target language of the Essay).
	Category 2: Studies of a Literary Works (at least one work written in the target language of the essay compared with works written in another language).
	Category 3: Studies in Language (all works originally produced in the target language of the Essay).
	Example: **SUBJECT:** English A, Category 3
	GROUP 2
	For Group 2 (language B) essays you will need to specify the Category (and sub-category if a Category 2 essay):
	Category 1: Language (when the focus of the essay is on language aspects of a given "text" or cultural context).
	Category 2: Culture and Society
	a. *Culture and Society* (when the focus of the essay is on the impact of a specific issue or event on the language chosen).

b. *General Culture* (when the focus of the essay is on a specified cultural artifact (or artifacts) specific to a country or community. See Chapter 1.2.1 on page 6 for more information on what constitutes an "artifact".

Category 3: Literature *(when the focus of the essay is on language types in a work or works produced in the target language).*

> *Example:*
>
> **SUBJECT:** French B, Cat 2 (b)

WORLD STUDIES

For world studies essays, you will need to indicate the:

a. chosen theme

World studies themes
• conflict, peace and security • culture, language and identity • environmental and/or economic sustainability • equality and inequality • health and development • science, technology and society

b. two subjects used in terms of the essay's methodological approach (for example, history and social and cultural anthropology).

> *Example:*
>
> **SUBJECT:** World Studies, Equality and Inequality, History and Economics

d. Word count	As of 2016, all Extended Essays will be digitally uploaded for assessment. This means the word count can more easily be ascertained by examiners so you must ensure that you accurately specify the **exact number of words** contained in your Extended Essay on the title page before uploading it for assessment. See page 131 for more detail on what counts as part of the total word count and what does not.
DO NOT INCLUDE:	Your name, school's name, candidate number or any identifying pieces of information on the title page (or any other section of the essay such as headers or footers). As the work is uploaded, the IB tags the work to your digital profile so these details are not required on the essay itself. What's more, in order to maintain the integrity of this externally assessed work, the IB does not disclose your name to examiners so it is essential you do not include any identifying marks within the essay itself.

Table of contents

All Extended Essays must contain a table of contents placed **after** the cover page and before the introductory section of your essay.

The table of contents should contain **a sequential list** of all your essay's sections or chapters. Next to each section or chapter heading should be the page number where that section or chapter begins. These page numbers should be placed on the far right of the page as indicated in the example below:

Chapter or sections should use numbers or letters (that is, Section A).

Table of Contents

Page numbers are aligned on the right-hand side of the page.

Sub-chapters (or sections) are indented and numbered.

If you use letters instead of numbers for your headings the sub-chapters can be numbered thus: i) ii) iii) iv) and so on or A.1, A.2 and so forth.

Question and Answer

Question: Do all Extended Essays need to have a table of contents?

Answer: Yes. Even in the case of language A Extended Essays, where the normal expectation is for continuous prose as opposed to sections (and sub-sections), a basic table of contents should be provided even if it simply has introduction, main body and conclusion as its key sections.

Page numbers

Page numbers should be included on all pages of the Extended Essay though convention dictates that a page number is not required on the title page and table of contents. You will not be penalized, however, if they do contain page numbers.

It does not matter which format you choose (for example, 1, 2, 3 ... Page 1, Page 2 and so on) or where the page numbers are located (for example, at the bottom right or in the centre). Ideally, aim to have the page numbers at the bottom of the page rather than the top.

Ensure the page numbers referred to in the table of contents match those in the body of the essay. You will lose marks if your table of contents states that Chapter X begins on page 5 when in fact it begins on page 6.

Fonts

The IB does not specify which font to use, however, it is mandatory that the font chosen is easily readable. You should not, therefore, use cursive, floral, cartoon or similar designer fonts that would make the script difficult to read.

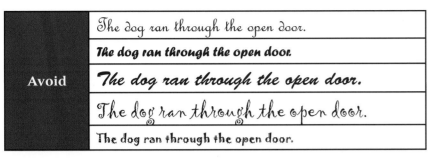

	The dog ran through the open door.
Avoid	**The dog ran through the open door.**
	The dog ran through the open door.
	The dog ran through the open door.
	The dog ran through the open door.

Preferred fonts include:

| Arial | Times New Roman | Calibri |

FONT SIZE: The IB now mandates that the font size should be **12pt.** If you wish to emphasize a word or heading, do not use a larger font, instead use **bold** (or capitalization for headings).

Spacing

As part of the Presentation criteria, it is mandatory to **double space** your essay. This allows examiners to insert annotations when marking it while also making for a smoother reading experience.

If you are using MS Word (PC), the spacing option appears here:

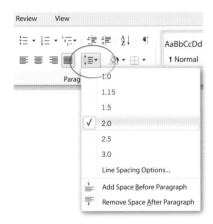

Referencing (citations and bibliography)

Referencing is a key skill that all IB (and university) students must master early on in order to produce work that meets accepted academic norms while simultaneously avoiding issues relating to academic malpractice. (For more see Chapter 8: Academic honesty, pages 139–43.)

| Note |
| Referencing the work of others is mandatory for all IB assessments. |

In a nutshell, the provenance (origin) of any work you use that is not of your own making or thought processes must be accurately referenced so as to acknowledge its source. It is a means by which you show indebtedness to the work others have done in your chosen area or topic while simultaneously acting as a platform from which you can base your own ideas and develop your own lines of argument.

Failure to do this could lead to the non-award of a grade for the Extended Essay (or any IB assessment), and thus could jeopardize your chances of securing an IB qualification. This means that learning how to correctly reference is perhaps one of the most vital skills you will need to learn.

In some instances, your own work will also need to be cited if it is used as authoritative material (for example, a table of data based on an experiment you've conducted or fieldwork you completed for any other assessments or assignments).

Referencing basics

a. **Reference:** Is the acknowledgment of the provenance of the work(s) that you've used in any written work that is not of your own making.

b. **Citation:** An in-text citation means to reference a work directly where it appears in your text by referring to the most basic source information (usually the surname, year of publication and page number where applicable though this will vary based on the style chosen (for example, MLA does not require the year for in-text citations)).

> *Example:*
>
> *...was not an accurate representation as "Basil's golden legacy was relatively short lived" (Holmes, 2006, p.4).*

In-text citation (APA style)

c. **Footnote:** A space at the bottom of the page where you can place a more complete reference. The reference is indicated in-text by an elevated number. Bear in mind, you do not need to include an in-text citation and footnote. Choose one approach that works for you and stick with it throughout your Extended Essay.

> *Example:*
>
> *... that according to Holmes was not an accurate representation as "Basil's golden legacy was relatively short lived".[1]*

Footnote numbering

Tip

You can use Microsoft Word to automatically insert footnotes into a document (see pages 123–8).

The insert Bibliography feature will allow you to embed the full reference as a footnote also.

Don't forget to include the page number(s) in the footnote (where available).

---

[1]Holmes, C. (2006). *Basil II and the Governance of Empire (976–1025)*, Oxford Studies in Byzantium, 1st Edition. Oxford: Oxford University Press, p.4.

Footnote including all reference details and page number(s) using APA style.

d. Citation style: This is the arrangement of provenance (origin) details in relation to an accepted citation system. There are many accepted citation styles (Oxford, Harvard, MLA, APA and so on). By and large, they have minor stylistic differences between them (mostly the order of details or use of abbreviations as can be seen in the examples below).

Examples:

American Psychological Association (APA)

Holmes, C. (2006). *Basil II and the Governance of Empire (976–1025),* Oxford Studies in Byzantium, 1st Edition. Oxford, England: Oxford University Press, p.4.

Modern Languages Association (MLA)

Holmes, Catherine. *Basil II and the Governance of Empire (976–1025).* Oxford Studies in Byzantium. 1st Edition. Oxford, England: Oxford University Press, 2006, p.4.

Some subjects have a preference for a specific style over another (for example, literature and language essays prefer MLA whereas psychology-based essays prefer APA).

The IB, however, **does not** prescribe a particular citation style so you are free to choose one that works for you (or that is followed by your school as a whole). What is important, however, is that you use one and adhere to that particular style throughout your work (don't mix and match styles!).

Question and Answer

Question: What do I need to cite?

Answer: Nearly everything that was written or produced by someone else or that acts as an authoritative basis for points raised in your essay (see below).

Type of writing	Cite?	Details
Direct quotes (word for word copy) from texts or internet sites.	Yes	Place the citation after the quote.
Paraphrasing or summarizing someone's work	Yes	Place the citation after the sentence or paragraph where the paraphrasing ends or immediately after the author's name if used in-text.
Images	Yes	Place the citation in a caption at the bottom of the image. This applies to adapted images also or specific details of images. In these instances adding the words "adapted from" or "detail of X" followed by the full citation details is necessary.
Dictionary definitions	Yes	As with direct quotes.
Common expressions	No	If using idioms or proverbial sayings there is no need to cite. However, if the word or phrase is coined by a particular individual as a means to communicate a key point in their work, then you must cite the source (for example, if I encounter the word "Tsunamail" in an article on the internet about the overuse of workplace emails and I choose to use it in my essay, I should acknowledge its original source).

Common knowledge	No	Commonly known pieces of information such as the fact that water is made of two molecules of hydrogen and a molecule of oxygen or the Pythagorean equation do not require a citation. However, how many goals X football player scored or the distance between Earth and Sun will require a citation as these specific pieces of information would not classify as common knowledge and thus require authoritative backing by way of a citation.
Copyright-free material	Yes	"Copyright free only" refers to the fact that you can use the material without having to pay a royalty or licence fee. It does not mean you avoid citing the source, however.
Music and films	Yes	Just like texts, all work not of your own making must be cited (including screen shots or sections of score).
Letters	Yes	Even personal letters a member of your family wrote would require a citation if they have been used in your essay.
Maps, diagrams, illustrations, tables, graphs and so forth	Yes	Even when you adapt them and add your own layers or work to them you should acknowledge the base source. In all cases you should label these as Figure 1 or Table 1 and so forth in the caption followed by the title and year of production. If you refer to these in the body of your essay (in-text) simply write "see Figure 1" (or whichever label you used in the caption).
My own maps, diagrams, , illustrations, tables, graphs and so on	Yes	If you use data that you generated yourself for some other assignment or assessment and intend to use it as an authoritative source upon which to base your analyses in the essay then you should cite your own work (for example, Lekanides, K., "Oxygen Levels as a Percentage of Total Mass in Picnic Point Topsoil" [Table], 2015, Own Data). The raw data can be added in an appendix.
My own images	Yes	As with images in general, you can cite your own if they are used as part of the essay.

A useful rule of thumb to operate by when it comes to citations is that if you are in doubt as to whether or not some information you've included requires a citation, cite it anyway. You cannot be penalized for "over-citing", but you can be penalized for not citing.

> **Golden rule:** If in doubt, cite.

e. Exemplar references

Below are examples of what a citation should look like for a variety of different source types. For convenience, all examples utilize the APA style unless otherwise specified.

i. Books

Citation

…that according to Holmes was not an accurate representation as "Basil golden legacy was relatively short lived" (Holmes, 2006).

Bibliography

Holmes, C. (2006). *Basil II and the Governance of Empire (976–1025)*, Oxford Studies in Byzantium, 1st Edition. Oxford, England: Oxford University Press.

ii. Websites

Citation

... it was not uncommon to see "overall infection rates of 15%" (D. Robson, 2008) among prisoners of war in the Far East ...

Bibliography

D. Robson, E. Welch, NJ. Beeching, G.V. Gill (2008, October 14). *Consequences of Captivity: Health Effects of Far East Imprisonment in World War II*. Retrieved September 24, 2015, from QJM: An International Journal of Medicine, Oxford University Press: http://qjmed.oxfordjournals.org/content/102/2/87

iii. Interviews

Citation

... children express difficulties in relation to "the rules of interaction such as initiating, maintaining and terminating the topic of conversations" (Pags, 2014) to the point where they ...

Bibliography

Pags, M. (2014, June 21). Social Pragmatic Interaction. (K. Lekanides, Interviewer)

iv. Images

All images used in an Extended Essay should appear as near as possible to where you first reference them in the text. The images should contain a fully referenced caption as seen below:

APA Style

Fig. 1: *Mona Lisa*

Vinci, L. D. *Mona Lisa*. La Gioconda. Musée du Louvre, Paris.

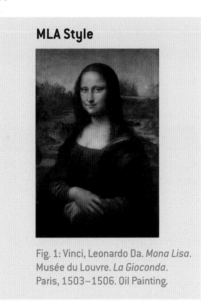

MLA Style

Fig. 1: Vinci, Leonardo Da. *Mona Lisa*. Musée du Louvre. *La Gioconda*. Paris, 1503–1506. Oil Painting.

Note

The key difference between APA and MLA is the latter includes the year the work was produced and its medium (type). APA generally requires the heading to go above the image.

If the image is from an internet source, include the date (day, month, year) accessed and URL.

Citation

... the fantastical background which acts as the backdrop for Da Vinci's Mona Lisa (see Fig. 1) was reputed to have been inspired by ...

Bibliography (APA style)
Vinci, L. D. Mona Lisa. *La Gioconda.* Musée du Louvre, Paris.

Bibliography (MLA style)
Vinci, Leonardo Da. *Mona Lisa.* Musée du Louvre. *La Gioconda.* Paris, 1503–1506. Oil Painting.

➢ Own image

If using an image you created, the same rules apply as above. Ensure you include your name, title of image, year of production, type (for example, photo, painting and etching)) and location.

v. Tables and graphs

Figure 1: IB Diploma candidate growth by region

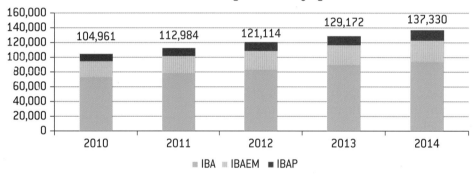

The IB Diploma Programme Statistical Bulletin, May 2014 Examination Session, IBO, 2014 [Graph]. Retrieved September 21, 2015, from IBO: www.ibo.org/contentassets/bc850970f4e54b87828f83c7976a4db6/may-2014-stats-bulletin.pdf

> **Note**
>
> If using a table, "Figure 1" should be replaced with Table 1, Table 2 and so on otherwise the information to be included is the same.

Citation

... policies that seem to have resulted in a steady growth of about 8,000 IB students from 2010 to 2014 (see Figure 1) ...

Bibliography
IBO. (2014). *IB Diploma Statistical Bulletin, May 2014 Examination Session.* Retrieved September 21, 2015, from IBO: www.ibo.org/contentassets/bc850970f4e54b87828f83c7976a4db6/may-2014-stats-bulletin.pdf

F. Bibliography (or works cited)

For the purposes of the Extended Essay, you are expected to include **only** works that you've actually cited in the body of the essay in your bibliography.

In this sense, a more accurate way of looking at it is as "Works Cited" rather than an all-encompassing Bibliography of all the works you read.

As with citations, the style does not matter provided you stick with one throughout. A useful tool to help you generate accurately formatted bibliographies (and citations) is available in Microsoft Word (see pages 121–8 for more).

As a minimum, the IB expects that your bibliography contains the following pieces of information:

Minimum expectations
● Author(s) name
● Publication date
● Title
● Page numbers (for print material)
● Date accessed (for online material)

Tip

Do **not** include works in your bibliography that are not cited in the main body of the essay or you will lose marks from Criterion D (Presentation).

How to add citations and bibliographies using Microsoft Word on a PC

Part 1: Adding sources

Step 1. Go to "References" and select "Manage Sources".

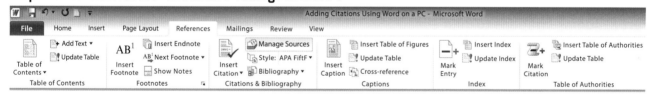

Step 2. Select "New" to add a new source to your "library".

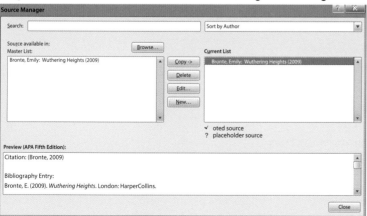

Step 3. Choose the type of source you would like to add to your "library". Then fill in the required areas.

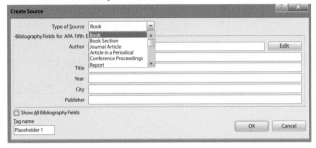

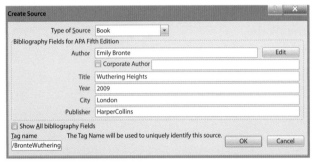

Step 4. Press "OK" and your source should now be added to your library. Note: You must press "copy" to add your Source to the "Current List" that you are using for a particular piece of work.

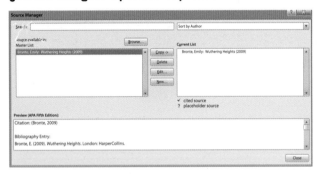

Part 2: Adding citations to your essay

Once you have written your quote or added your image, you can add a citation by going to "References" and choosing "Insert Citation". Then select the source that the quote came from.

You should have now succesfully inserted a citation!

For Vatherine and Heathcliff, love and punishment will always intermingle. Theirs is a tormented love that would probably not do well under peaceful circumstances. They seem to thrive on drama. "She was much too fond of Heathcliff. The greatest punishment we could invent for her was to keep her separate from him: yet she got chided more than any of us on his account" (Bronte, 2009).

Part 3: Adding a bibliography

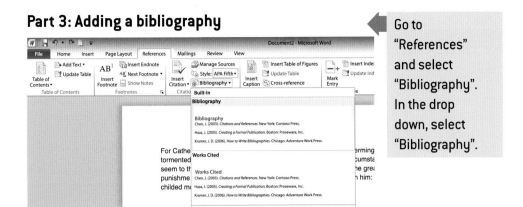

Go to "References" and select "Bibliography". In the drop down, select "Bibliography".

You should now have a bibliography. Do check to make sure there are no typos or errors.

Bibliography

Bronte, E. (2009). *Wuthering Heights*. London: HarperCollins.

Payne, E. (2011, September 26). *Lady Gaga Attends Obama Political Event*. Retrieved August 12, 2015, from CNN: http://edition.cnn.com/2011/09/26/showbiz/gaga-obama-fundraiser/

How to add citations and bibliographies using Microsoft Word on a Mac

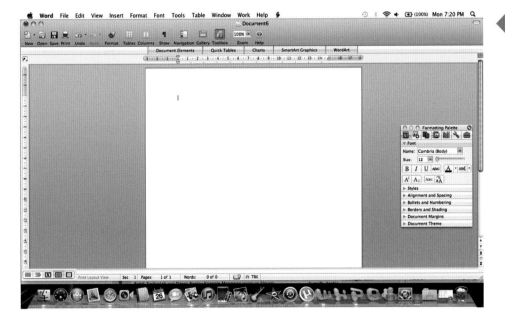

Open Microsoft Word: Select "Document Elements".

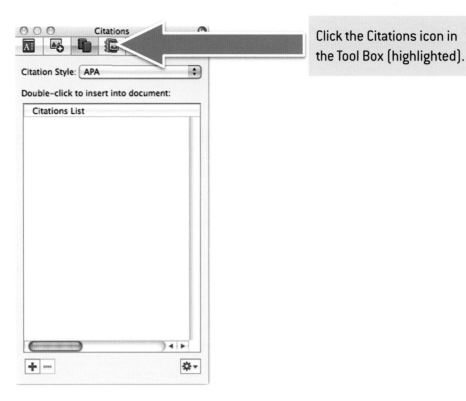

Click the Citations icon in the Tool Box (highlighted).

Open the drop-down box as shown and click "Citation Source Manager...".

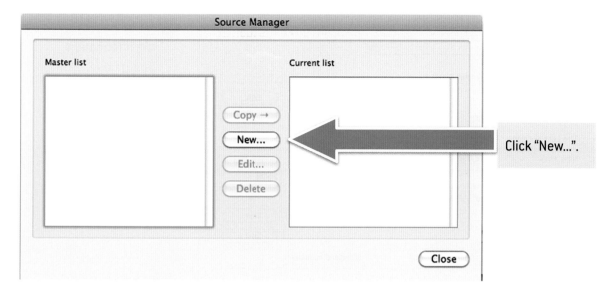

Click "New...".

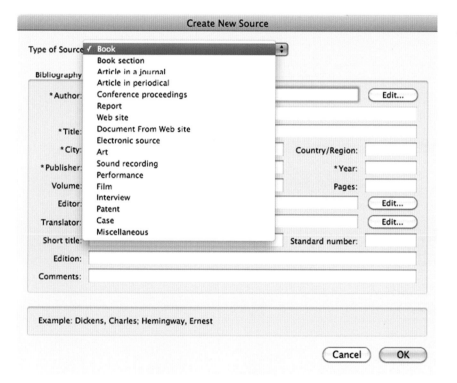

Open the first drop-down box and choose your source accordingly.

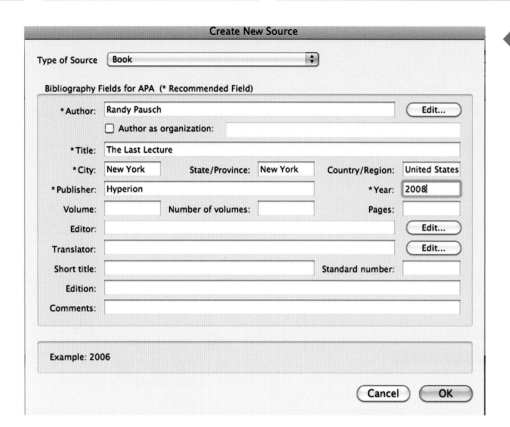

Fill in the rest of the information about your particular source and then click OK.

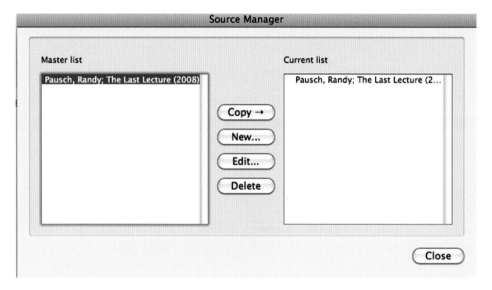

Click "Copy" so it is also inserted in your "Current List" and then "Close".

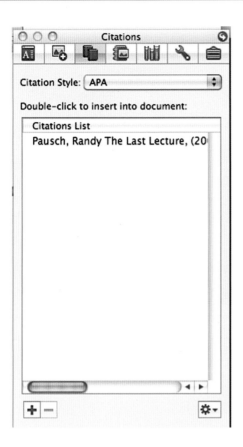

It will now appear in your Citations Tab in your Toolbox as seen below.

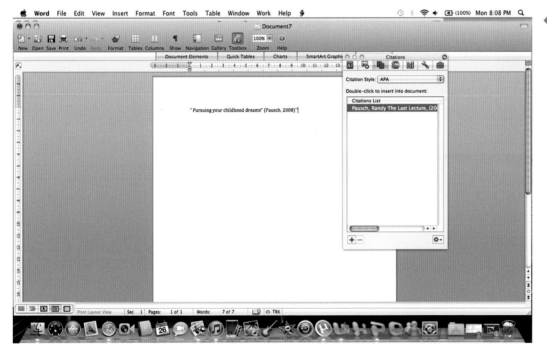

Put your cursor on the point where you want to insert your reference, and double click your Citation.

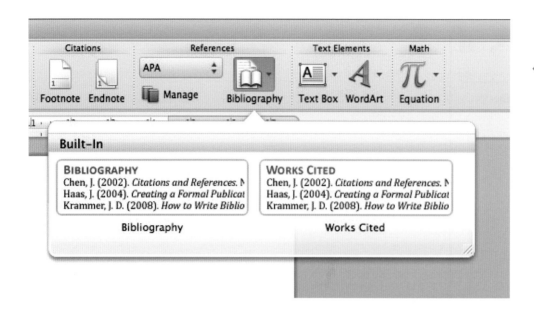

Click on "Bibliography" under the Reference tab. Format the bibliography based on the style and font of your document.

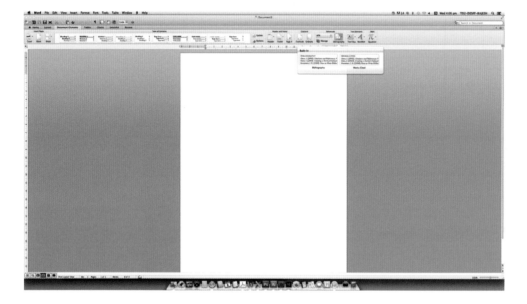

Bibliography information sheet

Below is a worksheet you can use to gather the relevant pieces of
information for a variety of sources. Each of these should be included
in your bibliography, where applicable. For how to organize the
information, refer to the examples on pages 118–20.

Books	
Author(s) name(s):	
Title:	
Year of publication:	
City:	
Publisher:	
Website	
Author(s) or institution:	
Webpage (name of the page you cited the information from):	
Website (the webpage's host):	
Date produced (year minimum):	
Date accessed (day, month, year):	
URL:	
Interview	
Interviewee:	
Title or topic (of interview):	
Interviewer:	
Date (day, month, year):	

Image or art

Author (if any):	
Title:	
Institution (museum, gallery, digital site and so forth)	
City (where located):	
Publication date*:	
Medium (type of work)*:	

* If using MLA style you will require both the production date and medium in addition to the other details.

Graphs and tables

Author(s) or institution:	
Title:	
Publication date (year minimum):	
Date accessed (day, month, year):	
Publication name (for example, journal) or URL:	

Film

Title:	
Director:	
Year:	

| Performers*: | |
| Medium*: | |

* If using MLA style you will also need the list of main performers (actors) and medium (for example, DVD or CD) on which the film was viewed.

Word count

The absolute maximum amount of words that an Extended Essay can be is **4,000**.

It is vital that you do not exceed this upper word limit as it will not only lose you marks in Criterion D (Presentation) but across all criteria as examiners will stop marking anything after the 4,000 word limit mark. This includes any analyses, arguments or concluding comments you've added.

Question and Answer

Question: What is included in the word count?

Table 1: Adapted from the IB Extended Essay Guide, 2016

Included	Not included
The introduction, all sections of the main body and the conclusion	Table of Contents
All quoted material	Maps, charts, diagrams, tables or illustrations including their accompanying caption or heading Note, however, that if any of the above contain commentary or analysis that will be counted.
Any footnotes (or endnotes) that are not citations or references. That is to say, any explanatory text or definitions or similar material that is added in a footnote will count as part of the word count.	Equations, formulas and calculations
Inclusion of multiple units of measurement. For example, if you write the temperature as 25°C and also place the measurement in Fahrenheit next to it—that is, 25°C (77°F)—then this will count as two words.	In-text parenthetical citations, for example (Rees, 2015)
Anything in parentheses that is not a citation such as dates, alternate spellings of names, definitions, descriptions and the like will count.	The Bibliography or "Works Cited" section of the Extended Essay
Chapter headings (and sub-headings)	The Reflections on Planning and Progress Form
	All material placed in Appendices Note: Examiners are not obliged to read any material in appendices so if you include material that is vital to the development of your essay it should be in the main body of the essay and not in an appendix.

Presentation checklist	Tick
Title page	
1. Does your title page contain a title generated from your research question?	
2. Does the research question on the title page match the one in other parts of your essay?	
3. Does the conclusion answer the research question on the title page?	
4. Is the spelling and grammar of the research question correct?	
5. Does the research question end with a question mark?	
6. Is the subject (or subjects if world studies) mentioned on the title page?	
7. Have you included the Category (and sub-category if applicable) on the title page for Group 1 or 2 Extended Essays?	
8. Have you included an accurate word count on the title page?	
9. Have you ensured that no personal information is on the title page?	
Table of contents	
Does the Essay contain a table of contents?	
10. Is the list of sections or chapters sequential (that is, as they appear in the essay)?	
11. Do the page numbers in the table of contents correspond to the right pages?	
Page numbers	
12. Does every page have a page number on it?	
Fonts	
13. Does the essay use a readable font (Arial, Times New Roman or Calibri)?	
14. Is the font size set to 12pt?	
Spacing	
15. Is the essay double spaced?	
Referencing (citations and bibliography)	
16. Does the essay include citations (either in-text or in a footnote/endnote format) using an approved style (such as APA or MLA)?	
17. Does the essay include a bibliography of only the works cited in the body of the essay?	
18. Does the bibliography adhere to one style (such as APA or MLA)?	
19. Is the bibliography in alphabetical order?	
20. Is the spelling of all words in the bibliography correct?	
21. Do images, tables, graphs and so forth have captions that include all reference details?	

Criterion E: Engagement (6 marks)

This criterion has two key strands associated with it:

| Process | Research focus |

What is being assessed under this criterion is your engagement with both the research process and focus of your investigations (or topic).

How is this assessed?

The way the IB assesses this criterion is by means of the Reflections on Planning and Progress Form (RPPF) which has been newly introduced alongside the current criteria. In this form you will be expected to write three reflections after having met with your supervisor at each of three key junctures in the Extended Essay Process. The supervisor's report that is added to the RPPF will also shed light on how well you've engaged with the two strands for this criterion.

There will inevitably be more than three sessions with your allocated supervisor where you cover a wide variety of things in support of your Extended Essay. These sessions will range from quick 10–20 minute meetings to longer sessions to go over your research plan or provide feedback on your draft.

The three mandatory reflection-specific sessions, however, will ideally be as follows:

1. First reflection session
- This will be one of the early sessions with your supervisor (not necessarily the first) where you will outline your ideas regarding the topic in general, the research question you have in mind, initial background reading or research you may have conducted, possible approaches and your initial thoughts about the answer to your research question.

2. Interim reflection session
- This session will usually fall somewhere in the middle to latter half of your EE calendar, usually before the first full draft is completed. The general expectation is that you are able to present to your supervisor a more refined RQ, discuss your essay on the basis of some sustained writing and comment on any challenges encountered and what solutions you've attempted.

3. Final reflection session (viva voce)
- This session is indeed the last time you will meet your supervisor as it is intended to be the closing interview. This session takes place after the EE is uploaded for assessment so your supervisor will have read your work. It is an opportunity to offer your final reflections on the process, discuss any achievements and challenges overcome, while also sharing any aspects that contributed to the completion of the essay but are not immediately apparent within it.

How many words can I write in the RPPF?

The form is a fillable PDF and is restricted to **500 words** in total, so an economy of relevant and sharply focused summative words is in order. An example RPPF can be found on page 138.

What do I need to bring to the Reflection Sessions?

The IB advises all students to maintain a Researcher's Reflection Space (RRS) for the purposes of supporting them with both their research and as evidence to show how well they've engaged with both the research focus and process overall. The RRS can be kept in any form (for example, journal, scrapbook or online blog). It is intended to be a place where the process is chronicled as a whole and can therefore be a showcase to your supervisor of your level of engagement with the Extended Essay as a whole.

Towards meaningful reflection

Reflecting before, upon and after action has proven time and time again to be a key ingredient to successfully creating any "product", be it a piece of homework, a creativity, activity, service (CAS) activity or an Extended Essay.

But why do we reflect?

The reason we reflect could be broadly separated into five categories:

Discerning pros and cons

EE link: What are the advantages or disadvantages of my chosen approach?

Adjusting action

EE link: What should I do to counteract problems or limitations with my research approach?

Gap filling

EE link: What is missing from my research or analysis? What else should I be doing?

Re-evaluating goals

EE link: What is my research pointing to that differs from my initial hypothesis or position? Has my research focus changed?

Celebrating failure

EE link: What have I learned from my mistakes or choices made as part of my research? How successful was I in overcoming them?

So what is good reflection?

Although this will vary from situation to situation, broadly speaking it is safe to say that good and poor reflecting will be characterized by the following features:

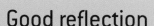

Good reflection

- meaningful
- individual
- ongoing and episodic
- formative
- corrective
- uncomfortable
- productive
- social
- challenging

Poor reflection

- descriptive only
- complaining
- criticizing only
- boring
- linear or static
- politically correct
- tick box
- hour counting
- a single task

Good reflecting should challenge you, your assumptions and your approach. It should be social in nature as you seek to find solutions to problems through dialogue and discourse with experts. Good reflecting should always correct bad practice or erroneous steps in your research. It should be an ongoing process and generally episodic in nature rather than a one-off task you complete at the end. Most importantly, it should be meaningful, by which is meant it should help you realize what worked and what didn't and thus point you towards finding appropriate solutions or support.

How can I reflect?

All students should create a "space" where they can keep notes, clippings from useful articles, video files, annotations, scribbled ideas and anything that helps build the Extended Essay.

What form this "space" takes is completely up to you.

A traditional approach is to keep a running journal with clippings and annotations (much like a scrapbook only that the focus is your Extended Essay's research question). However, you should not be limited to this, especially when you have access to a myriad of digital platforms and spaces that can help contain and exhibit your work.

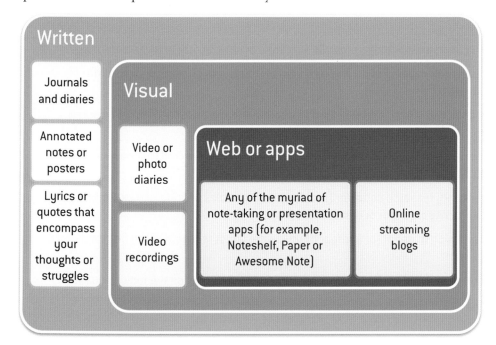

What should I include in my Researcher's Reflection Space (RRS)?

The key to making this space work is to include:

- **Reading:** A log of your reading as you complete it. (This could be in the form of a bibliography and/or some short notes on what you thought you gained from each source, even if minimal to non-existent! Remember, good reflection acknowledges mistakes made or incorrect paths followed.)

- **Notes:** Brief notes on your developing (often changing) thoughts on your RQ as a result of your reading and research

- **Challenges:** Register any challenges (even frustrations) and what you did about them, especially if they revolve around the research itself. Avoid simply complaining about things such as missed opportunities or time wasted. Reflect on how you can avoid these issues in future.

- **Visuals:** Include annotated diagrams, charts, illustrations or images that help build your argument.

- **Skills:** Document any newly developed skills or refining of pre-existing skills that you gain as a result of the research process.

Getting the most out of reflection

Below is a list of key questions that you should consider when writing your core reflections in your Researcher's Reflection Space which could then inform what you end up including in the assessed Reflections on Planning and Progress Form (RPPF). Each key question below is subdivided into additional stimuli questions to help guide your reflections along a more research focus. Bear in mind that you do not need to answer all of the additional stimuli questions as they may not all apply to you. What you must do, however, is respond to the key questions as a minimum. Your supervisor should encourage questioning along these lines so you can make the most out of those meetings.

Key question
1. How effective were your choices?

    a. In what way(s) did your chosen methodology produce a definite or satisfactory answer to your RQ?

    b. In what way(s) did your personal reading shed any new light on the text or challenge, or confirm pre-existing schools of thought?

    c. In what way(s) did your choice of source material lead to a comprehensive assessment of (most) all factors?

    d. Was your choice of sources consistently relevant to your RQ? What implication did that have on your conclusion (for example, "it produced a more sharply focused conclusion").

    e. To what extent did your primary research consider (most) all key variables or factors in external agents (such as socio-cultural influences, gender or researcher bias)?

    f. To what extent did your research material (or approach) utilize the latest research in the field, making it up to date?

    g. In what way(s) did your research highlight any undocumented or new thoughts on the topic in question?

    h. To what extent could your approach be seen as yielding reliable (and/or valid) results?

2. What changes were necessary during the research process?

    a. Did your research bring to light any material or data that forced you to rethink your approach or adjust your RQ accordingly?

    b. Did your methodological approach or choice of sources consistently yield the required results or were changes/additions required?

    c. In what way(s) did your Extended Essay compel you to seek out new modes of note taking or overall organization (for example, time management)?

    d. To what extent did you include a wide variety of source material (that is, not just internet sources)?

    e. Did your argument require a greater balance of opinion that forced you to do wider reading or additional primary research?

    f. Why did you switch from a primary to secondary research approach (or vice versa)?

3. What were the greatest achievements and challenges during your research process?

    a. Did your research require you to acquire more technical skills or adapt your technical proficiencies so as to conduct your research properly (for example, learning how to use specific lab or technological equipment or how to devise subject-appropriate surveys)?

    b. Was there a lack of sufficient source material to begin with when it came to your topic? How did you overcome this?

    c. In what way(s) has your research findings added to the existing body of knowledge around your chosen topic?

    d. Did you make any significant breakthroughs with regards to the topic in question?

    e. Were you able to devise any original approaches to respond to your RQ?

    f. In what way(s) was your conclusion a comprehensive response?

    g. In what way(s) could your chosen topic or approach be deemed a challenge to research or pursue (for example, deals with complex mathematics, concerns itself with an obscure aspect of history or attempts a new reading of a well-known text)?

    h. Did you acquire any new skills that you have found use for in other areas of your studies?

Note

The RPPF is not intended to be a place where you mention any medical or personal problems you may have encountered. Any adverse circumstances will be communicated to the IB via your IB Diploma Coordinator through a different channel, so seek their guidance if that applies to you.

Exemplar Reflections on Planning and Progress Form

Below is an example of the kinds of things you could write in the three reflection spaces on the Reflections on Planning and Progress Form (RPPF). The key at all times is to maintain a focus on the process of researching and writing the essay itself.

The example is intended for a history Extended Essay but similar types of reflection could be raised with any subject.

RQ: To what extent could Anna Comnena's "Alexiad" be read as a criticism of the reign of Emperor Manuel I?

First reflection

- I was attracted to Anna Comnena's the *Alexiad* as a result of some extra readings that formed part of my IB history course (the Crusades). As the first female historian Comnena stands in a unique place in terms of historiography, something which appealed to me as both a woman and budding historian. I was initially considering writing about her accounts of the First Crusade but quickly found the topic to be far too wide in scope. A reading of Paul Magdalino's article "The Pen of the Aunt" helped refocus me on the issue of historical purpose, that is, why she wrote the history she did. I have now allocated time to reading historical accounts of Manuel I's reign to decide how closely the events Comnena mentions in her history of her father's reign (Alexius) so as to validate my current hypothesis that she intended the work to be a celebratory account of her father so as to cast a negative light on the rule of her nephew Manuel I. My current list includes, Runciman, France, Macrides, Christomides and Hill.

Interim reflection

- I was finding it hard to come up with a satisfactory counter to the questions of accuracy and authenticity that feature prominently in modern readings of her work. Historians ranging from Edward Gibbon and John France to the more direct Howard-Johnson paper that completely challenges her authorship effectively negated my hypothesis entirely. Using Magdalino and Hill as a focus point, I reread key sections of the *Alexiad* and mapped out her account against the political events of Manuel I's reign and quickly discovered some interesting overlaps (building works, military campaigns, relations with the West and so forth). Although occasionally obscure and subtle, the criticisms emerge by means of an unspoken comparison which Byzantine readers of her account would have well understood. This approach is providing me with a suitable counter to the aforementioned criticisms. I have also begun structuring my work accordingly with sections devoted to historical context followed by a section on the *Alexiad* that compares and contrasts events from Alexius' time with those of Manuel's. I am considering a chapter on the historiographical tradition of Byzantium but may integrate it into the main body in the end.

Final reflection

- I am very pleased with how the essay has turned out. Skills-wise, I had no problems with referencing, which I picked up quickly. However, integrating source analysis did prove a challenge at times due to my narrative tendencies. I believe I've been able to challenge the orthodox interpretations of Comnena's work as a piece of fantasy fiction at the hands of a disgruntled woman by showing that she was effectively using one of the few weapons she still possessed in her diminished political state—the power of words—to criticize the existing leadership. Hill's works proved of particular use to me as they examined female power in a broader context and thus gave me a framework for interpreting what Comnena was able to do within the context of her time.

8: Academic honesty

In 2011, Germany's youngest ever Defense Minister, Karl-Theodor zu Guttenberg, was forced to resign his post as a result of a plagiarsim scandal that had developed around his 2007 doctorate in law. It was discovered that large sections of the work contained uncited source material that put into question its authenticity and, one could argue, the integrity of its author.

Karl-Theodor zu Guttenberg

What this, and many other similar stories, highlights is that **academic honesty matters**. It is not something that the IB takes lightly, nor is it something that any student at any level of education or in the professional sphere should ignore.

What is academic honesty?

Being academically honest effecively means being able to stand behind all your produced work as genuinely stemming from your own efforts. Where you have relied on or used other people's work you have acknowledged this and no fabrication of data is present.

What does the IB consider academic malpractice?

The IB considers academic malpractice to have occurred when:

- a student has committed **plagiarism**, that is to say, used the ideas or work of another and passed it off as their own

- a student allows another to use or submit their work as his or her own. This is called **collusion** and is most often seen when students allow others to copy their homework or sections of a previously submitted assessment. This also applies to students submitting work that was already submitted by a student from a different year group.

- a student **duplicates the same work** for different assessments or in order to meet different diploma requirements

- a student **cheats** in an exam

- a student **fabricates or falsifies** data (for example, lies in their CAS record or makes up the statistics for a science Extended Essay).

(adapted from Diploma Programme: Academic Honesty, IBO, 2011, p.3)

Plagiarism

Plagiarism is by far the most common form of academic malpractice that students commit, especially when it comes to longer pieces of writing such as is the case with the Extended Essay. This is not always malicious in intent but rather the by-product of a lack of insight or understanding as to what exactly counts as plagiarism and what does not.

The following section aims at helping students identify what constitutes plagiarism through a worksheet of real-life scenarios so that they are able to avoid committing it when the time comes to writing their Extended Essay.

Also refer to Chapters 3 (pages 45–48) and 4 (pages 58–60) that contains information on evaluating source reliability and conducting a literature review. This is often useful in helping to ensure that the information used from sources (especially web-based ones) is reliable to begin with.

So what counts as plagiarism?

Aspect	Notes
1. Direct quotes (written and oral)	Any words that are used exactly as they were written or said by another must be adequately cited.
	Quotation marks ("X") at the beginning and end of the quoted material and an in-text citation or footnoted reference are required.
	For example:
	According to Smith, "this was an event of unparalleled magnitude" (Smith, 2009) as it ushered in a period of ongoing conflict.
	The spoken word is of particular interest as it is often assumed that it is exempt and there is no need for a citation but this could not be further from the truth.
2. Paraphrasing	Paraphrasing (or rewriting) someone else's ideas, views, theories or words (spoken or written) in your own words is considered plagiarism unless adequately cited.
	An in-text citation or footnoted reference after the section where you've borrowed someone else's ideas is required.
	For example:
	This act by Genghis Khan was of an unprecedented scale as it ushered in a period of ongoing conflict between the Persians and Mongols (Smith, 2009).
3. Factual Information	Any facts, statistics, graphs, illustrations, tables and so forth that was borrowed by someone else (written or oral) must be cited.
	Even when a student feels they know quite a lot of factual information about a topic (for example, how many goals Cristiano Ronaldo scored in certain matches) they should still cite a source as it is good academic practice to back-up your data with some form of external validation.
	This does not apply, however, to things that could be deemed *common knowledge* such as who was America's first African-American President, when World War I broke out or how many molecules of hydrogen there are in water.
	If in doubt as to whether something is or isn't common knowledge, remember the golden rule: **when in doubt, cite**.

Plagiarism test

Below are a series of real-life scenarios that one encounters when having to decide whether to cite material or whether it is acceptable not to. Your task is to select what the correct response is to each situation.

> Remember the Golden Rule:
>
> ## When in doubt, cite.

Note

Answers with explanations can be found on page 143 so that you can check your own responses once you're done.

Scenarios
1. You read an article in the *Discover Magazine* and you recall a bunch of facts that you use in a homework essay you are writing.

Should you:	Cite	☐	Don't Cite	☐

2. You downloaded a JPG image from the internet and used it in one of your assessments.

Should you:	Cite	☐	Don't Cite	☐

3. You encounter the phrase "best thing since sliced bread" in a novel and use it in one of your own writing tasks.

Should you:	Cite	☐	Don't Cite	☐

4. You find the perfect image for your Extended Essay on the internet. The fine print reads "copyright free".

Should you:	Cite	☐	Don't Cite	☐

5. You interview your grandfather about his experiences during the Falklands War and include aspects of these in your background chapter in your history Extended Essay.

Should you:	Cite	☐	Don't Cite	☐

6. You've been a passionate fan of Lionel Messi for many years. You are able to reel off facts and statistics and retell gaming highlights from memory. You write a report on your childhood hero.

Should you:	Cite	☐	Don't Cite	☐

7. You encounter the term "tsunamail" in an article that perfectly captures the flood of emails one receives on a daily basis. You use this term in your essay.

Should you: Cite ☐   Don't Cite ☐

8. You find the exact sentence "Water is made up of two molecules of hydrogen and a single molecule of oxygen" in more than 100 websites. You use this phrase in your biology essay.

Should you: Cite ☐   Don't Cite ☐

9. You use background information from a Japanese language magazine and use self-translated ideas from it in your English essay.

Should you: Cite ☐   Don't Cite ☐

10. You contact an artist whose work you wish to use in one of your assessments and he gives you permission in an email.

Should you: Cite ☐   Don't Cite ☐

11. You write a paragraph made up of no more than 10 words taken from a variety of sources that you've joined together to form a new whole.

Should you: Cite ☐   Don't Cite ☐

12. You write a paragraph using ideas from a history book. You directly quote one sentence from the source which you place within inverted commas and include an in-text citation after it.

Is this: Plagiarism ☐   Not Plagiarism ☐

PLAGIARISM TEST ANSWERS (from pages 141–2)

1. Cite

Factual information that is not common knowledge should be referenced as standard practice.

2. Cite

Images that have been taken from the internet were not of your making and therefore they must be fully acknowledged.

3. Don't cite

Idiomatic expressions are part of the common vocabulary of all languages and thus do not require citation even if read in other works.

4. Cite

Copyright free means that no royalties need to be paid to the original creator, but this does not mean you should not cite the image (or work). Copyright free refers to financial considerations not referencing ones. The same rule would apply to copyright free music, artwork and illustrations.

5. Cite

Oral retellings of events require adequate citations just like textual versions. It may often help to cite these as interviews.

6. Cite

Although the details are well-known to you personally, this does not mean they are common knowledge. Factual information that is not common knowledge should be referenced as standard practice. It is also good academic practice to support any factual information with external sources that help validate the information you've used.

7. Cite

This term is coined by the person in the article and it has not yet become common usage (as opposed to words such as "Google" and "selfie") and therefore it should always be cited.

8. Don't cite

Basic definitions or factual references that fall into the category of common knowledge (for example, "photosynthesis is a process that occurs in plants", "George Washington was the first president of the USA" and "the First World War broke out in 1914") do not require citing. However, if the phrase includes a specific turn of phrase or details that differentiate it from the commonly accepted basic form, then you should cite.

9. Cite

Just because the text does not appear in English this does not mean you should not cite the original used from the Japanese source. This applies to all languages. Students need to be extra careful to not assume that their text will not be spotted even if they are using their own personal translation.

10. Cite

You would still need to cite the source as permission (written or oral) and provide proper academic referencing.

11. Cite

Even though you've created a pastiche of ideas and borrowed words and created something "new" from it you are still required to acknowledge all your original sources by way of recognizing that this work is formed out of other people's ideas.

12. Plagiarism

This is plagiarism because it only references (cites) the direct quote as opposed to the entire paragraph which freely borrowed ideas from the original source. You must be careful to not forget that paraphrasing needs to be accurately cited in addition to direct quotations.

1.3 Extended Essay quiz answers

1. b **2.** c **3.** a **4.** c

5. b **6.** d **7.** d **8.** c

9. a **10.** d **11.** d **12.** a

Index